Seeds
OF
Peace

Seeds OF Peace

A Catalogue of Quotations
Compiled by
Jeanne Larson & Madge Micheels-Cyrus

new society publishers

Philadelphia, PA   Santa Cruz, CA

Inquiries regarding requests to republish all or part of *Seeds of Peace* should be addressed to: **New Society Publishers, 4527 Springfield Avenue, Philadelphia, PA 19143, USA.**

ISBN: 0-86571-098-8 Hardcover
0-86571-099-6 Paperback

Printed in the United States of America on partially recycled paper.

Cover graphic by Kathy Fox; Design by Mike Holderness.

This book was compiled as a project of **Waging Peace, PO Box 383, Hayward, WI 54843, USA.** A portion of the proceeds of this book goes to support the work of Waging Peace, a resource collective committed to creative peace education.

To order directly from the publisher, add $1.50 to the price for the first copy, 50¢ each additional. Send check or money order to: **New Society Publishers, PO Box 582, Santa Cruz, CA 95061, USA.**

New Society Publishers is a project of the New Society Educational Foundation, a nonprofit, tax-exempt, public foundation. Opinions expressed in this book do not necessarily represent positions of the New Society Educational Foundation.

Quotations from *Christ in a Poncho* by Adolfo Pérez Esquivel, © 1983 English translation. Reprinted by permission of Orbis Books.

Quotations from *Food First News* are reprinted with the permission of Ann Kelly, Publications Director of Food First, Institute for Food and Developmental Policy, San Francisco.

Quotations from *Johnny Got His Gun* by Dalton Trumbo, © 1969, Introduction Addendum copyright 1970. Reprinted by permission of Carole Stuart, Publisher, Lyle Stuart, Inc.

Quotations from *Meet Mr. Bomb: A Practical Guide to Nuclear Extinction*, © 1982, edited by Tony Hendra, published by Larry Durocher. Reprinted with permission of Larry Durocher, High Meadows Publishing, Inc.

Quotations from *Nuclear Winter* by Carl Sagan, © 1983. Reprinted by permission of Carl Sagan.

Quotations from *Cosmos* by Carl Sagan, © 1980. Published by Random House, Inc., NYC. Reprinted by permission of Carl Sagan.

Quotations from *Our Future at Stake: a Teenager's Guide to Stopping the Nuclear Arms Race*, © 1984 by Melinda Moore and Laurie Olson. Reprinted with the permission of the Citizens Policy Center Nuclear Action for Youth Project.

Quotations from *Please Save My World*, © 1984, edited by Bill Adler. Reprinted with the permission of Arbor House.

Quotations from *We Won't Go: Personal Accounts of War Objectors*, collected by Alice Lynd, © 1968 by Alice Lynd. Reprinted by permission of Beacon Press.

Quotations from the *Winter Soldier Archives*, an introduction to *The Short-Timer's Journal, Soldiering in Vietnam No. 1*, © 1980. Reprinted by permission of Clark Smith of the Winter Soldier Archive.

Contents

For our children
(Jamila, Jay, Tamra, Tanya & Zachary);
their children;
their children's children;
their children's children's children...

Preface

The words in this book contain a lot of *power*. It is the same kind of power that is found in a seed....Power that makes a small plant germ take hold on an inhospitable rock ledge and grow there into a sturdy tree....Power that causes tender green plants to rise up out of dark graves and break through a blacktop crust.

The words in this collection are powerful like that. We think that they deserve to be circulated widely. That is why we have created this resource, making over 1600 *seeds of peace*—quotations on war, peace, nonviolence and images of a peaceful world—available under one cover.

There are two main parts to the book: quotations on "Waging War" and quotations on "Waging Peace." Three smaller parts are found in the center section: "The Lighter Side of a Serious Subject"; "Patriotism"; and "Bumperstickers, Buttons, T-Shirts and Graffiti."

How to use the book

Like garden seed catalogues that serve both the committed and casual gardener, this catalogue of quotations has many uses. Those who write speeches, articles, sermons and newsletters will find "seed thoughts" in here. The user who wishes to find a quotation for a specific purpose will be aided by the book's 29 chapter headings and by the complete index. The purpose of the book is also served by a random sampling of the quotations. For every time a word about peace is read or spoken, a thought of peace stirred, or an image of peace created in the mind, we believe that activity alone brings peace a little closer. The quotation book will be "waging peace" every time it is used.

Within each chapter, the quotations are arranged to "tell a story." We found that persons who lived a century apart sometimes echoed one another's thoughts precisely. We have paired such quotations in the book. Sometimes it was the striking contrast between two perspectives that caught our attention and led us to put quotations together. In every case, we believe that the order of the quotations in the book will contribute to creative stirring of thought.

Direct sowing or composting?

Many of the quotations in the book are like seeds of peace that are suitable for "direct sowing." That is especially true of the quotations that are found in the "Waging Peace" section. Most of the quotations in

Part I, "Waging War," however, are of another variety. Those thoughts are not "plantable" so much as they are "compostable." These quotations first need to be composted in the thought process of the mind—where they can be decomposed, recycled and converted from death talk into ideas and images that support life.

What about sexist language?

In working on the seedbed of this project, we came across one big "rockpile." And that was what to do about the sexist language in many of the quotations. The more we worked on the book, the more aware we became of the power of words. (No wonder Edward Robert Bulwer-Lytton claimed that "the pen is mightier than the sword"!) What, then, to do about words that address everyone as male; words that exert their power in the direction of reinforcing sexism in society?

At first, there was no doubt in our minds. Where sexist language was used, we had to make what changes were necessary to make it inclusive language. Otherwise, we would be giving wider circulation to words that perpetuate the "power over" mentality that gives rise to a war and violence mentality. That would be defeating our purpose of waging peace by producing this book!

It was one thing to conclude that sexist language had no place in our book. Figuring out exactly what to do about it was another matter.

Should we change the sexist words to inclusive terms in the quotation with footnotes citing how it appeared in the original text? Should we italicize the sexist words (or put them in parentheses) to indicate that something is out of order there? Should we put the inclusive language term in parentheses alongside the sexist word used in the original text? Should we take the sexist language out of those quotations where it can be done so practically, and leave it in where it would require too much re-writing? Can we legitimately change a word, even if we do document the change? Should we do nothing in the text and urge the user to deal with the problem? Can we legitimately do nothing? How about offering two versions of each sexist quotation—the original and an inclusive language re-write—much like a bi-lingual text?

...We struggled!... What would you do, for example, with a quotation like this: "Can anything be more ridiculous than that a man has a right to kill me because he dwells on the other side of the water, and because his prince has a quarrel with mine, although I have none with him?" (Blaise Pascal, *Pensées*, IV)

We found that we could not address the sexist language word for word in quotations like this—be it with italics, parentheses, or footnotes—without unacceptably affecting the integrity and readability of the quotation.

We eventually reached our decision about what we would do with the recognition that there was no solution that would be 100% satisfactory—to us, or to every user of the book. To do nothing would insult readers whose patience with the use of sexist language has run out. To make changes of any kind would offend those whose literary and editorial ethics insist that no changes whatsoever of any kind for any reason can be made in an original text.

What we have done is this:

* Wherever an asterisk appears at the beginning of a quotation, we have determined that gender has been used in a sexist way in that quotation.

The asterisk is intended to serve as a "warning flag," encouraging the reader to be on the look-out for:

—gender-exclusivity in that quotation;

—the need for inclusive language adaptations whenever possible in the use of the quotation.

We found that there was one encouraging note about all the difficulty we had with the issue of sexist language. And that is that not many years ago, it would not have been an issue. That it was a problem for us now bears witness to the fact that basic cultural changes do take place. If our attitudes toward language can change, why not our attitudes about war and peace?

Sowing what you want to reap

...Finally, this book of seeds needs you, the sower, to become useful. We are confident that in your hands it will be a valuable tool for moving toward the harvest of peace that we all desire.

Jeanne Larson
Madge Micheels-Cyrus
October 1986

Acknowledgements

"...Did Beethoven do the dishes? Did Mozart sweep the floor?" These questions, posed in a folk song by Ginny Reilly and David Maloney, point to the reality of invisible support structures that make visible accomplishments possible.

Seeds of Peace clearly represents the efforts of more than two people.

It represents an accomplishment of Waging Peace, a unique support structure. We could not have composed this resource in our spare time alone. We had more than spare time to devote because peace work is our part-time wage work. We are hired by peers who want to see employment opportunities added to the volunteer work force in order to escalate the total peace effort. It is not only a lot of work that is represented here, but also a lot of *will*—will for peace on the part of the supporters of Waging Peace. The book in your hands is a testimony to that will and the power of what can be accomplished by it.

In addition, financial support has come from Jackie Rivet-River and Louis River, from the Division on Social Concerns of the Northwest Association and the Commission on Social Concerns—both of the Wisconsin Conference, United Church of Christ, and from the Church and Society Committee of the Presbytery of Northern Waters, Presbyterian Church (USA).

Others to be thanked for their help are our Waging Peace colleague Tom Hastings, who contributed prize quotes and picked up office chores, Sunshine Jones, Gerri Williams, Shelley Anderson and Jeanne Audrey Powers for their input on the problem of sexist language, Michael Skindrud for his clarification, Margaret and John Lintula for proofreading, Grandma and Grandpa Kanicky for helping out at home and with the youngest child, and Jack and Lynn whose support, literally, included washing dishes and sweeping floors.

Seeds of Peace is truly a collective accomplishment....May we propose a toast to us all?

Publisher's Note

Brief quotations and epigrams can have a powerful—and unpredictable—effect on our consciousness: often more powerful than whole books or even conversations. As someone who works with words, who is even unfashionably committed to the written word, I often have cause to wonder how often anyone's mind has ever been changed by reading. I suspect rarely: far more likely that reading something which is timely and sums up one's own part-formed thoughts will cause those thoughts to crystallize, to become active and powerful. This is, I hope, the potential of this book: among the almost overwhelming number of quotations here there may be one or two which will at a given time reach you personally, or which will reach audiences you are addressing. They may be phrases which remind us of the hope and beauty in the world, or those which remind us of what must be overcome.

When in the early Seventies I first came across the slogan *Nous sommes tous des juifs Allemands*: "We are all German Jews"—on a poster from the near-uprising in Paris of May 1968—I was disturbed and puzzled. The slogan made me stop and think. It was clearly a clever play on Kennedy's *Ich bin ein Berliner* (in which he unwittingly placed himself on a *Delikatessen* shelf—but that's another story). It seemed to be dramatising the *potential* for massive violence of the State, with its tanks at the ready on the outskirts of the city. But was it an irresponsible use of shock value? Did it trivialise the Holocaust?

In 1979, as I became immersed in the literature of Nagasaki and Hiroshima and cruise missiles, that slogan came back to me and made a great deal of sense—though perhaps not the sense that the presumed author, running off overnight posters on a silk-screen in some Paris basement, had in mind. We *are* all German Jews. We are *all* Communists and Gypsys and homosexuals. Sitting fearfully through the days after the bombing of Libya, startled by the flash of lightning or the wail of a ship's siren, feeling utterly powerless: is this how it felt in the Warsaw ghetto in 1941, in a Berlin hideout in 1937? Yet for me the image of that quotation is not—now—one of desperation. For opening ourselves to the depth of our predicament must be a part of changing it. When I am asked what I, as a pacifist, would have done against Hitler, I must answer: "Start earlier! Not start opposition when it was too late, in 1939 or 1941, but in 1920 or 1923..." We, in acting against a new Holocaust of all the earth's people, can start as soon as we like: now.

As much as this could be written about any quotation in this book. It may be that others will affect you in ways that their original authors, writing in other times, never imagined. It is probable that some quotations were not first uttered by those credited here; this is not an academic reference work. It *is* a "thought tool," a crystal seed for your thoughts and those of people around you.

Mike Holderness

1
Militarism

* Man has no right to kill his brother. It is no excuse that he does so in uniform; he only adds the infamy of servitude to the crime of murder.

Percy Bysshe Shelley

Soldiers are taught to consider arms as the only arbiters by which every dispute is to be decided....They are instructed implicitly to obey their commanders without enquiring into the justice of the cause they are engaged to support; hence it is, that they are ever to be dreaded as the ready engine of tyranny and oppression.

Joseph Warren, 1772

* Once a man enters the army, he is expected only to follow the heels ahead of him.

Carson McCullers

* A crew-cut captain greeted us with these words: "What does k-i-l-l spell?" "Kill," was the obvious, though not too loud, reply of most of the three hundred voices..."I can't hear you!" "Kill!" A deafening chant began: "Kill! Kill! Kill!..." I looked around me. Clerks, mechanics, teachers, college students, a few professional men, all were screaming, "Kill!" Who cares who? Just kill. Kill anyone that the President, the Congress, and the generals brand as "evil," "aggressors," "the enemy"....

As I look back, I cannot condemn these men, or those who went before or now follow them. Very few of these men are inherently cruel, depraved, or deranged. But fear, power, and hatred are the order of the day, and it is to these forces, so constantly presented to us both by demagogues and by those who should know better, that men submit without question. Good men do bad things because they are too benumbed to ask "Why?" or say "No!" Our society, but particularly the military, demands men who will follow without thinking.

Stephen Fortunato, Jr.
We Won't Go

If my soldiers began to think, not one would remain in the ranks.

Frederick the Great

If you would remain men be not soldiers; if you do not know how to digest humiliations, do not put on the uniform.

Jean Grave
Dying Society and Anarchy

* Humilities are piled on a soldier...so in order that he may, when the time comes, be not too resentful of the final humility—a meaningless and dirty death.

John Steinbeck
East of Eden

I can use up 25,000 men a month.

Napoleon Bonaparte, 1798

* The military has an almost metaphysical concept of its power and righteousness; the military demands that the individual abandon his reason and his conscience in a supreme and "patriotic" act of self-abnegation in order that he might proudly assume his niche in an invincible mass of manpower and machinery that will—to use military terms—"close with the enemy and destroy him."

Stephen Fortunato, Jr.
We Won't Go

* Man is the only Patriot. He sets himself apart in his own country, under his own flag, and sneers at the other nations, and keeps multitudinous uniformed assassins on hand at heavy expense to grab slices of other people's countries, and keep *them* from grabbing slices of *his*. And in the intervals between campaigns he washes the blood off his hands and works for "the universal brotherhood of man"—with his mouth.

Mark Twain

* Just as it would be stupid to plant weeds and try to harvest vegetables, so it would be stupid to encourage the lies, conscription, and murder of war, and hope to produce democracy, freedom, and brotherhood.

Dave Dellinger
on entering prison, 1943

Never think that war, no matter how necessary, nor how justified, is not a crime. Ask the infantry and ask the dead.

Ernest Hemingway

* Killing one man constitutes a crime and is punishable by death. Applying the same principle, the killing of ten men makes the crime ten times greater and ten times as punishable. Similarly, the killing of a hundred men increases the crime a hundred fold, and makes it that many times as punishable. All this the gentlemen of the world unanimously condemn and pronounce wrong. But when they come to judge the greatest of all wrongs—the invasion of one state by another—(which is 100,000,000 times more criminal than the killing of one innocent man) they cannot see that they should condemn it. On the contrary, they praise it and call it "right." Indeed, they do not know it is wrong.

Moh-tze
3rd Century B.C.
Courage in Both Hands

* Justice is as strictly due between neighbor nations as between neighbor citizens. A highwayman is as much a robber when he plunders in a gang as when single; and a nation that makes an unjust war is only a great gang.

Benjamin Franklin, 1785

* Can anything be more ridiculous than that a man has a right to kill me because he dwells on the other side of the water, and because his prince has a quarrel with mine, although I have none with him?

Blaise Pascal
Pensées, IV

It has been argued that, when killing is viewed as not only permissible but heroic behavior sanctioned by one's government or cause, the fine distinction between taking a human life and other forms of impermissible violence gets lost, and rape becomes an unfortunate but inevitable by-product of the necessary game called war.

Susan Brownmiller

I would no more teach children military training than teach them arson, robbery, or assassination.

Eugene V. Debs

* Now children are very pretty, very lovable, very affectionate creatures (sometimes); and a child can make nitro-glycerine or chloride of nitrogen as well as a man if it is taught to do so. We have sense enough not to teach it; but we do teach the grown-up children. We actually accompany that dangerous technical training with solemn moral lessons in which the most destructive use of these forces at the command of kings and capitalists is inculcated as heroism, patriotism, glory, and all the rest of it.

George Bernard Shaw

He had grown up in a country run by politicians who sent the pilots to man the bombers to kill the babies to make the world safe for children to grow up in.

Ursula K. LeGuin
The Lathe of Heaven

We've gained from the wars a lot of trouble and hatred and bitterness.... Women are for peace always. They are for peace by nature.

Jehan Sadat

Nowhere have women been more excluded from decision-making than in the military and foreign affairs. When it comes to the military and questions of nuclear disarmament, the gender gap becomes the gender gulf.

Eleanor Smeal
National Organization of Women

I'm certain that if a minority of women in every country would clearly express their convictions they would find that they spoke not for themselves alone but for those men for whom war has been a laceration—an abdication of the spirit.

Jane Addams
Nobel Peace Prize, 1931

War has shown that government by men only is not an appeal to reason, but an appeal to arms; that on women, without a voice to protest, must fall the burden. It is easier to die than to send a son to death.

Mary Roberts Rinehart
Kings, Queens, and Pawns

We have always borne part of the weight of war, and the major part....Men have made boomerangs, bows, swords, or guns with which to destroy one another: we have made the men who destroyed and were destroyed. We pay the first cost of all human life.

Olive Schreiner

As a woman, I can't go to war and I refuse to send anyone else...You can no more win a war than you can win an earthquake.

Jeannette Rankin
only Congressperson to vote against
US entrance into both World Wars

I want to stand by my country, but I cannot vote for war. I vote no...The world must finally understand that we cannot settle disputes by eliminating human beings.

Jeannette Rankin

It does not follow that if women will vote, they must fight, for war is not the natural state of the human family.

Elizabeth Cady Stanton

* It is sometimes said that war is a natural condition of man. As a military man, I do not believe it.
 I do believe breathing, eating, loving, caring, are natural conditions of man. People don't make war, governments do.
 And our governments appear willing to accept war, even nuclear war, as a natural event.
 There is not one nation in the world where the people want war.

Rear Admiral Gene R. La Rocque
U.S. Navy (retired)

In peace, children inter their parents; war violates the order of nature and causes parents to inter their children.

Herodotus

Hear me, my chiefs, I am tired. My heart is sick and sad. From where the sun now stands I will fight no more forever.

Chief Joseph
Nez Percé, 1877

Revenge by young men is considered gain, even at the cost of their own lives, but old men who stay at home in times of war, and mothers who have sons to love, know better.

Chief Seattle, 1859

I am tired and sick of war. Its glory is all moonshine. It is only those who have neither fired a shot nor heard the shrieks and groans of the wounded who cry aloud for blood, more vengeance, more desolation. War is hell.

General William Tecumseh Sherman, 1879

There is many a boy here today who looks on war as all glory; but, boys, it is all hell. You can bear this warning voice to generations yet to come. I look upon war with horror.

General William Tecumseh Sherman, 1880

War is sweet to those who don't know it.

Desiderius Erasmus

* I have known war as few men now living know it. Its very destructiveness on both friend and foe has rendered it useless as a means of settling international disputes.

General Douglas MacArthur

War is, we have been forced to admit, even in the face of its huge place in our own civilization, an asocial trait...if we justify war, it is because all peoples always justify the traits of which they find themselves possessed, not because war will bear an objective examination of its merits.

Ruth Benedict
Patterns of Culture

As long as war is regarded as wicked it will always have its fascinations. When it is looked upon as vulgar, it will cease to be popular.

Oscar Wilde
Intentions

War, to me, is the greatest weakness of all.

Anaïs Nin

The guns and the bombs, the rockets and the warships, all are symbols of human failure.

Lyndon B. Johnson

Throughout history there has never been an evitable war. The greatest danger of war always lies in the wide-spread acceptance of its inevitability.

James P. Warburg

The possibility of a short and decisive war appears to be one of the most ancient and dangerous of human illusions.

Robert Lynd

* War has persisted because...men have made an exception of each particular war and gone out to mutual slaughter.

Jesse Wallace Hughan

Wars will cease when men refuse to fight—and women refuse to approve. Do not allow people to lead you to think for a moment that war is a necessary institution.

Jesse Wallace Hughan

General, your tank is a mighty machine. It shatters the forest and crushes a hundred men. But it has one defect: It needs a driver.

Bertolt Brecht

* The pioneers of a warless world are the young men who refuse military service.

Albert Einstein

War will exist until that distant day when the conscientious objector enjoys the same reputation and prestige that the warrior does today.

John F. Kennedy

* Weapons are instruments of fear; they are not a wise man's tools...
Peace and quiet are dear to his heart,
And victory no cause for rejoicing.
If you rejoice in victory, then you delight in killing;
If you delight in killing, you cannot fulfill yourself.

Lao Tsu
Tao Te Ching, **Thirty-One**

On happy occasions precedence is given to the left,
On sad occasions to the right.
In the army the general stands on the left,
The commander-in-chief on the right.
This means that war is conducted like a funeral.
When many people are being killed,
They should be mourned in heartfelt sorrow.
That is why a victory must be observed like a funeral.

Lao Tsu
Tao Te Ching, **Thirty-One**

To rejoice in conquest is to rejoice in murder.

Lao Tsu

The next dreadful thing to a battle lost is a battle won.

Wellington

* The problem after a war is with the victor. He thinks he has just proven that war and violence pay. Who will teach him a lesson?

A. J. Muste

After all, war isn't that effective. In every case, at least one side loses, which is only 50% effective, if you're lucky. The winner pays a very large price, as well.

Gene Sharp

There never was a good war or a bad peace.

Benjamin Franklin

Nothing is lost by peace; everything may be lost by war.

Pope Paul VI

We are ready to kill to keep our automobiles running. We're ready to kill to keep up our materialistic, wasteful economy...I am sick and tired of 18-year-olds being coerced into bearing the burden of the failure of politicians to face the tough economic choices needed to end our dependency on foreign oil.

Mark Hatfield
Senator, Oregon

I spent thirty-three years and four months in active military service....And during that period I spent most of my time being a high-class muscle man for big business, for Wall Street and for the bankers. In short, I was a racketeer, a gangster for capitalism...I helped make Mexico safe for American oil interests in 1914. I helped make Haiti and Cuba a decent place for the National City Bank boys to collect revenue in. I helped purify Nicaragua for the international banking house of Brown Brothers...I brought light to the Dominican Republic for American sugar interests in 1916. I helped make Honduras "right" for American fruit companies in 1903. Looking back on it, I might have given Al Capone a few hints.

Major General Smedley Butler, USMC
New York Times interview, August 1931

When we were in Grenada, I really enjoyed myself. You were out there with your gun, shooting, taking prisoners, doing everything Marines are supposed to do.

Lance Corporal Gordon Brock

Patriots always talk of dying for their country, and never of killing for their country.

Bertrand Russell

The master class has always declared the wars; the subject class has always fought the battles.

Eugene Debs

Those who can't find anything to live for always invent something to die for. Then they want the rest of us to die for it, too.

Anonymous

* Government consists merely of professional politicians, a parasitical and anti-social class of men. They never sacrifice themselves for their country. They make all wars, but very few of them ever die in one.

H. L. Mencken

Militarism has been by far the commonest cause of the breakdown of civilization.

Arnold Toynbee

You can't say that civilizations don't advance, for in every war they kill you in a new way.

Will Rogers

Technological progress has merely provided us with more efficient means for going backwards.

Aldous Huxley

America has become a militaristic and aggressive nation...We have an immense and expensive military establishment, fueled by a gigantic defense industry, and millions of proud, patriotic, and frequently bellicose and militaristic citizens...Militarism in America is in full bloom and promises a future of vigorous self-pollination...unless the blight of Vietnam reveals that militarism is more a poisonous weed than a glorious blossom.

General David M. Shoup
Retired Marine Corps Commandant

Our whole social organism is riddled by the disease of militarism; and just as it seems that cancer can only be cured at the level of the organism as a whole, so we cannot hope to root out militarism without a similarly holistic therapy.

Rudolf Bahro

Show me who makes a profit from war, and I'll show you how to stop the war.   **Henry Ford**

This country is in the early years of the most expensive military boom in history. The expansion in military science and technology is the most ominous component of a defense budget that is dense with the ghosts of past and future wars.   **Emma Rothschild, MIT**
in the *New York Review of Books*

Profits are springing, like weeds, from the fields of the dead.

Rosa Luxemburg

The American military-industrial complex...was the real winner of
World War II.   **David Dellinger**

...we will never have peace...so long as people go on manufacturing
death and trying to sell it.
                                                    Edna St. Vincent Millay

The most disadvantageous peace is better than the most just war.
                                                        Desiderius Erasmus
                                                              Adagia

It is always immoral to start a war.
   Diplomatic and other non-violent means should always be used to
resolve conflicts and fend off aggression.
   If non-violent methods fail, and one nation unjustly attacks another,
the victim nation has as a last resort the right and duty to use violent
means to defend itself within certain moral limits.
   The military response to any attack may not exceed the limits of
legitimate self-defense.
   This means that the damage inflicted and the costs incurred must be
proportionate to the good expected by the taking up of arms. The
wholesale slaughter of civilians in large population centers is simply
immoral, whether the destruction is intentional or unintentional, direct
or indirect, no matter what weapons system is used.
         statement of the Catholic Bishops on the Just-War Theory

In the 1960's civilian and military deaths were about equal, but in the
last decade civilian deaths rose sharply. The average in the later period
is three civilian deaths to one battle death.
   Weapons fired from great distances are more destructive and
indiscriminate. Aided by mechanized equipment, conflicts fan out more
rapidly, destroying crops and food supplies, causing floods of helpless
refugees. Starvation takes many of them.
                                                      Ruth Leger Sivard

I am not proud of the fact that my son helped to bomb Vietnam....I
would like to go up to each one of them [the Vietnamese people] and
hold their hands in mine and say to them that I am sorry about the
bombing of their country, and I am terribly sorry that Jim was part of
it. It is not much, but what more can I say?
                                                        Virginia Warner
                                                   mother of a war prisoner
                                                 Winter Soldier Investigation
                                                          January 1971

The legacy of the Vietnam War is so sad, so riddled with frustration,
anger, and guilt, that it is easy to fall into the complacent attitude that
it is long over and best forgotten. But to forget that war has an immediate

hazard. Forgetfulness and complacency help renew the forces that are still in place that originally caused the war. However painful the truth of the war might be, it is preferable to myths, illusions, and rationalizations and their manipulation by those planning the next conflict.

Winter Soldier Archive

A murder medal. They give you medals for killing people.

Stephen Gregory
Bronze Star recipient
while sentenced for taking hostages in a Maryland bank in 1977

They want to call us heroes for serving the country. They offer us recognition and honor, even a national monument. Heroes for serving a country that burned down villages and shot anything that moved. Recognition for being the agents and pawns of a ruthless death machine that systematically tortured and butchered civilians, that rained flaming jelly gasoline and poison chemical gas on old men, women, and children. Receiving a past due debt of honor for using the most advanced, blood-curdling, and flesh-tearing weapons of terror the world has ever known. A monument for being the tools of a modern imperialist army that vainly attempted for over ten years to crush, grind and pulverize the people and land of Vietnam into the Stone Age, an army that finally sank to a well-deserved defeat at the hands of a just and determined peoples' war.

statement from Vietnam era veterans

Some 110,000 veterans have died since their return from Vietnam, twice the official number that died in combat. Many were suicides. When a man dies in combat from "friendly fire," his death can be listed as accidental. Many veterans whose deaths are officially recorded as accidental were really suicides. If the actual number is uncertain, it is certain the suicides from depression and aggravation stemming from the Vietnam experience is significant and continuing.

Winter Soldier Archive

The official line on the Vietnam war is that it was a "mistake." (Oops, 55,000 dead, another 35,000 "accidentally" killed, 33,000 crippled, 330,000 wounded.)

Winter Soldier Archive

What is missing in American life is a sense of context...in our journalism the trivial displaces the momentous because we tend to measure events by how recently they happened....We've become so obsessed with facts we've lost all touch with truth.

Ted Koppel

Numbers have dehumanized us. Over breakfast coffee we read of 40,000 American dead in Vietnam. Instead of vomiting, we reach for the toast.

Our morning rush through crowded streets is not to cry murder but to hit that trough before somebody else gobbles our share.

Dalton Trumbo
addendum to Introduction—1970
Johnny Got His Gun

An equation: 40,000 dead young men is 3,000 tons of bone and flesh, 124,000 pounds of brain matter, 50,000 gallons of blood, 1,840,000 years of life that will never be lived, 100,000 children who will never be born. Do we scream in the night when it touches our dreams? No. We don't dream about it because we don't think about it; we don't think about it because we don't care about it. We are much more interested in law and order, so that American streets may be made safe while we transform those of Vietnam into flowing sewers of blood which we replenish each year by forcing our sons to choose between a prison cell here or a coffin there.

Dalton Trumbo
addendum to Introduction—1970
Johnny Got His Gun

If the dead mean nothing to us (except on Memorial Day weekend...), what of our 300,000 wounded? Does anyone know where they are? How they feel? How many arms, legs, ears, noses, mouths, faces, penises they've lost? How many are deaf or dumb or blind or all three? How many are single or double or triple or quadruple amputees? How many will remain immobile for the rest of their days?... The Library of Congress reports that the Army Office of the Surgeon General for Medical Statistics "Does not have figures on single or multiple amputees." ...in the words of a researcher for one of the national television networks "the military itself, while sure of how many tons of bombs it has dropped, is unsure of how many legs and arms its men have lost."

Dalton Trumbo
addendum to Introduction—1970
Johnny Got His Gun

Vietnam has given us eight times as many paralytics as World War II, three times as many totally disabled, 35% more amputees...But exactly how many hundreds or thousands of the dead-while-living does that give us? We don't know. We don't ask. We turn away from them. We avert the eyes, ears, nose, mouth, face. "Why should I look, it wasn't my fault was it?" It was, of course, but no matter.

Dalton Trumbo
addendum to Introduction—1970
Johnny Got His Gun

When we pay our army and navy estimates, let us set down—so much for killing, so much for maiming, so much for making widows and orphans....We shall by this means know what we have paid our money for.

Anna Laetitia Barbauld, 1739

...All right, so we don't buy war as a concept. It's worse—we buy it in reality. On April 15 we all sent in our tax dollars— "Here," we said to our administration, "spend it wisely for me—go to the market and purchase what I need to make my life better." But we didn't give them a marketing list. And so those busy little budgeters put their heads together. And here we go again. Sixty-five cents out of every dollar for war—past, present, and future. Sixty-five cents out of every dollar for death and destruction.

Bess Myerson
You Don't Have to Buy War, Mrs. Smith
Mothers Day, 1970

Leftist extremist groups say they're using terror for the liberation of the people. But with terror you liberate nothing. State terrorists say they're practicing terrorism because their backs are to the wall—they've been forced into this "dirty war," and they're only using the same methods to defend what they call "Western Christian civilization." But they're not defending a thing! They're defending themselves and their shabby little interests, that's all. They're not defending the dignity of the human person. They're not defending the people.

Adolfo Pérez Esquivel
1980 Nobel Peace Prize
Christ in a Poncho

Terrorism is a label applied to certain criminal acts when the state doesn't like the criminal's politics.

Martin Oppenheimer

The issue is not one of good versus evil as Reagan would have it, but of violence versus nonviolence. On this score, the President has no moral standing to judge others, for he has bloodied his hands in Nicaragua, Lebanon, Grenada, and El Salvador. His proposed solution to stop terrorism by escalating state violence will only water the roots of terrorism.

The Progressive
Editorial—August 1985

Violence now is mainly organized and governmental.

Bertrand Russell

We often arrogantly feel that we have some divine messianic mission to police the whole world; we are arrogant in not allowing young nations

to go through the same growing pains, turbulence and revolution that characterized our history. Our arrogance can be our doom.
Martin Luther King, Jr.
March 1967

This peace loving nation has members of its armed forces stationed in 135 countries around the world—more than 100 troops in each of 25 countries.
Pentagon figures

If democracy is so good, why do we have to go to other countries and try to jam it down their throats with a gun? Stay here and make democracy work. If it's good you don't have to force it on others, they'll steal it.
Dick Gregory

...the idea that honor is flung away in peace, and retained in war, we would point out that inevitably the price of war includes honor....Democracy cannot co-exist with militarism.
Tracy D. Mygatt

You can't defend freedom; you must extend it.
James Bevel

* Even in the public military service, or warlike expeditions by national authority, the law manifestly requires the soldier to think for himself, to consider before he acts in any war, whether the same be just, for, if it be otherwise, the Common Law of the kingdom will impute to him guilty of murder.
Granville Sharp, 1773

* According to the Biblical narrative Adam sinned against God, and then said that his wife told him to eat the apple, while his wife said she was tempted by the devil. God exonerated neither Adam nor Eve, but told them that because Adam listened to the voice of his wife he would be punished, and that his wife would be punished for listening to the serpent. And neither was excused, but both were punished. Will not God say the same to you also when you kill a man and say that your captain ordered you to do it?
Leo Tolstoy

* And no action is more opposed to the will of God than that of killing men. And therefore you cannot obey men if they order you to kill. If you obey, and kill, you do so only for the sake of your own advantage—to escape punishment. So that in killing by order of your commander you are a murderer as much as the thief who kills a rich man to rob him. He is tempted by money, and you by the desire not to be punished, or to receive a reward. Man is always responsible before God for his actions.
Leo Tolstoy

* Shameful is the position of the prostitute who is always ready to give her body to be defiled by any one her master indicates; but yet more shameful is the pcsition of a soldier always ready for the greatest of crimes—the murder of any man whom his commander indicates.... And therefore if you do indeed desire to act according to God's will you have only to do one thing—to throw off the shameful and ungodly calling of a soldier, and be ready to bear any sufferings which may be inflicted upon you for so doing.

Leo Tolstoy

What makes this inquest significant is that these prisoners represent sinister influences that will lurk in the world long after their bodies are returned to dust. They are living symbols of racial hatreds, of terrorism and violence, and of the arrogance and cruelty of power. They are symbols of fierce nationalisms and of militarism.

Nuremberg Trials for Nazi leaders

* Crimes against international law are committed by men, not by abstract entities such as states, and only by punishing individuals who commit such crimes can the provisions of international law be enforced.
  That a soldier was ordered to kill or torture in violation of the international law of war has never been recognized as a defense for such acts of brutality....The true test, which is found in varying degrees in the criminal law of most nations, is not the existence of the order, but whether moral choice was in fact possible.

Nuremberg Tribunal judgment

* Hitler could not make aggressive war by himself. He had to have the cooperation of statesmen, military leaders, diplomats, and businessmen. When they, with knowledge of his aims, gave him their cooperation, they made themselves parties to the plan he had initiated....
  To initiate a war of aggression is...not only an international crime; it is the supreme international crime....

Nuremberg Tribunal judgment

ADDITIONS:

2
Facts of the Arms Race

For a deterrence to Russia…we need enough nuclear power to kill 1/4–1/2 of its population and destroy 1/5–1/4 of its industry. That would take 400 nuclear bombs. We have over 30,000.

1968 study commissioned by Robert McNamara
Secretary of Defense

There are now more than 50,000 nuclear weapons, more than 13,000 megatons of yield, deployed in the arsenals of the United States and the Soviet Union—enough to obliterate a million Hiroshimas. But there are fewer than 3000 cities on the Earth with populations of 100,000 or more. You cannot find anything like a million Hiroshimas to obliterate.

Carl Sagan
The Nuclear Winter

The essential fact remains that neither of the two superpowers can attack the other without signing its own death warrant. The Americans have at their disposal 40 nuclear warheads for each Soviet city of 100,000 and above. By comparison, the Soviets only have 15. But only one warhead is sufficient to do the job. That is why the two superpowers are more partners than they are adversaries. And that is why Europe is alarmed about a *de facto* equilibrium in which European territory is a possible theatre of nuclear operations without jeopardizing the homeland "sanctuary" of its protector.

General George Buis
former French Army Chief of Staff

The explosive power of nuclear weapons equals three tons of TNT for every individual in the world.

Jan Martenson
Under Secretary-General
Department of Disarmament Affairs, UN

The total firepower of World War II was three megatons. Today we have 18,000 megatons or the firepower of 6,000 World War IIs. The United States and the Soviets share this firepower with approximately equal destructive capability.

Freeze It!
A Citizen's Guide to Reversing the Nuclear Arms Race

There are nuclear devices so powerful that the explosive power of one is more than has been used since the invention of gunpowder.

Jan Martenson
Under Secretary-General
Department of Disarmament Affairs, UN

A so-called "limited" nuclear war could kill 22.7 million Americans, more than 20 times the total number of American dead and wounded in

World War II and 10 times the total American dead and wounded in all the wars in our nation's history.

Jerry Elmer
American Friends Service Committee

One modern submarine equipped with nuclear missiles can carry more explosive power than was used during World War II.

Jan Martenson
Under Secretary-General
Department of Disarmament Affairs, UN

...just two U.S. Poseidon submarines which carry 320 nuclear weapons can destroy all the 200 major Soviet cities with the destructive potential of 1,000 Hiroshima-size weapons.

Rear Admiral Gene R. La Rocque
U.S. Navy (retired)

If the nation continues with its current nuclear retaliation policy, ELF is not needed because of the nature of submarine communications. Under a first strike policy, it is essential.

Gene R. La Rocque

Together, Project ELF and the Trident Fleet will transform the U.S. submarine force from a deterrence posture, into the ultimate first-strike weapon system.

Robert C. Aldridge
former design engineer for Trident missile system

[The D-5 (Trident II Missile) would give the United States] pre- emptive capability. [The missile would have the] yield and accuracy to go after very hard targets [such as missile silos, which are heavily protected.]

Dr. Richard DeLauer
Under Secretary of Defense for Engineering
October 1981

Trident submarines:
...can carry up to 408 super-accurate Trident II warheads on each sub with each warhead having *five* times the explosive power of the bombs we dropped on Japan.
...have a range of 4,000 miles.
...cost $1.5 billion a piece, without its missiles.
Our country is planning to build over twenty Trident submarines.

ELF, Trident and You

The capacity to destroy 408 different cities or targets is a lot of death and destruction to put under the control of one submarine commander.

Robert C. Aldridge

MX Missiles:

...an ICBM (intercontinental ballistic missile) called "MX" (for "Missile Experimental.")

...71 feet long, 7 1/2 feet in diameter.

...carry ten Mark 12-A warheads of about 350 kilotons apiece. (The Hiroshima bomb was 12.5 kilotons.)

...100 meter accuracy.

...a counterforce weapon to attack missile silos and other hardened targets in the Soviet Union. (A counterforce capability has no practical value except in a first strike—MX warheads would fall on empty silos unless used first.)

...originally planned to be mobile on tracks. Now to replace old missiles in silos.

American Friends Service Committee

Nuclear tipped missiles place all of us but 30 minutes from Armageddon—tonight, every night, every hour of every day. There is no spot on earth assured of safety from obliteration. The maximum warning time is measured in minutes.

Dwight D. Eisenhower

The people of Hiroshima are separated from us by 40 years and half the world. They are still dying from the effects of that "small" bomb. Each cruise missile is 15 times as lethal as the bomb that was dropped on Hiroshima.

Alice Cook and Gwyn Kirk
Greenham Women Everywhere

Cruise missiles:

...small, pilotless, subsonic surface-to-surface missiles designed to fly under Soviet radar.

...are about 21 feet long.

...travel at 550 m.p.h. with a range of 1,500 miles and accuracy within 100–300 feet.

...have warheads in the 10–50 kiloton range.

...are not verifiable.

Greenham Women Everywhere

Pershing II missiles:

...are a two stage, mobile, surface-to-surface, ballistic missile.

...are 33 feet long.

...have a range of 1,130 miles and accuracy within 65–130 feet.

...carry one airburst/surface burst 10–20 kiloton warhead.

Defense Monitor
1983

The 1,000 mile flight from a base in West Germany to Moscow would reportedly take the Pershing II missile 6 minutes.

**Mark Hatfield
Senator, Oregon**

During a 10-month period, North American Defense Command had 151 false alarms due to mechanical and human errors which could have resulted in a nuclear catastrophe.

Dr. James Muller

The Soviet Union has said they will put their missile system on launch-on-warning of attack. Experts say Soviet computers are 5 years behind ours.

Anonymous

Space weapons would create a situation in which any satellite malfunction could be misinterpreted as the beginning of war. As satellites become more complex and their numbers increase, malfunctions will continue to occur. And as the amount of "space trash" increases, so does the likelihood of a random object hitting a satellite—and the likelihood of miscalculation and catastrophe.

Union of Concerned Scientists, 1983

The President wants Americans to believe that space weapons will "shelter" the entire population of the United States from nuclear attack...despite the fact that the government's own scientific studies show that unless these weapons are 95% effective (an inconceivably high level of performance), a minimum of 100 million Americans will die instantly in a blazing firestorm in the event of all-out nuclear war.

Dr. Benjamin Spock

...an effective defense of our population is technologically unattainable because it can be so easily countered by the Soviets. In addition, any [space based] Ballistic Missile Defense (BMD) systems can be outflanked by using low-flying cruise missiles and short-range, submarine-launched weapons. Thus, it will encourage the construction of more offensive weapons, not less, and bring a new escalation of the arms race.

Union of Concerned Scientists

The projected cost of the BMD system is astounding. The Reagan Administration has asked Congress for twenty-five billion dollars merely to demonstrate the feasibility of the technology over the first five years. The total cost to develop and deploy the system has been estimated at half a trillion.

Union of Concerned Scientists

...such development [BMD] would require the United States to violate or to repudiate the 1972 Anti-Ballistic Missile Treaty. This would be the first such "abrogation" of an arms treaty by a superpower since the dawn of the nuclear age.

Union of Concerned Scientists

It is particularly important that [Star Wars] research be carried out in a manner fully consistent with the ABM Treaty. To ignore such treaty restraints would encourage Soviet disregard for it on a scale that would dwarf our current concerns about their compliance.

Elliot L. Richardson
former Secretary of Defense

There are those who would seek to raise false alarms—by saying for example, that the Soviet Union has more ships than we do. But the fact is, you do not compare numbers. You compare total firepower, you compare tonnage and combat capability—and you find we are on top.

Gerald Ford

There is too much pessimism about our current capability. I would not swap our present military capability with that of the Soviet Union, nor would I want to trade the broader problems each country faces.

General David Jones
Chairman, Joint Chiefs of Staff
February 1979

By most relevant measures, we remain the military equal or superior to the Soviet Union.

Harold Brown
former Secretary of Defense
February 1980

It is naive to believe that the Russians will play by our rules any more than we will accept theirs. It is naive to believe that they—any more than we—would willingly accept a position of second best in military strength.

Cyrus Vance
former Secretary of State
June 1980

In the central region of Europe, a rough numerical balance exists between the immediately available non-nuclear forces of NATO (including France) and those of the Warsaw Pact.

Harold Brown
former Secretary of Defense
January 1980

I can confirm in all responsibility that a rough parity in strategic nuclear arms, medium-range nuclear weapons, and conventional armaments exists between the Soviet Union and the United States, and between the Warsaw Treaty and NATO.

Dmitri Ustinov
former Defense Minister, USSR
November 1981

What's the difference whether we have 100 nuclear submarines or 200? I don't see what difference it makes. You can sink everything on the ocean several times over with the number we have and so can they.

Admiral Hyman G. Rickover
January 1982

The United States is the dominant military and economic power not only in that [Pacific] theater but also in every other theater in the world.

Admiral Robert Long
Commander in Chief U.S. Forces, Pacific
March 1982

The Soviets do not have, in my judgement, anything like strategic superiority in the sense of a militarily or politically usable advantage in strategic nuclear forces.

Harold Brown
former Defense Secretary
April 1982

Not in one single nuclear weapons category have the Soviets demonstrated technological superiority. We have more strategic nuclear weapons than the Soviet Union. But you never hear this because the myth of U.S. inferiority is being spread to try and panic the public.

Herbert Scoville
former Deputy Director for Research, CIA

On balance the Soviet Union does have a definite margin of superiority—enough so that there is a risk and there is what I have called, as you know several times, a window of vulnerability....the Soviet's great edge is one in which they could absorb our retaliatory blow and hit us again.

Ronald Reagan
March 1982

[When asked by Senator Charles Percy: "Would you rather have at your disposal the U.S. nuclear arsenal or the Soviet nuclear arsenal?"] I would not for a moment exchange anything, because we have an immense edge in technology.

Caspar Weinberger
Secretary of Defense, April 1982

The United States and the Soviet Union are roughly equal in strategic nuclear power.

Department of Defense
Annual Report, 1982

...we must remember that it has been we Americans who, at almost every step of the road, have taken the lead in the development of [nuclear] weaponry. It was we who first produced and tested such a device; we who were the first to raise its destructiveness to a new level with the hydrogen bomb; we who introduced the multiple warhead; we who have declined every proposal for the renunciation of the principle of "first use"; and we alone, so help us God, who have used the weapon in anger against others, and against tens of thousands of helpless noncombatants at that.

George Kennan
former US Ambassador to the USSR

About 30 countries have already begun installing nuclear reactors. In twenty years, 100 countries will possess the raw materials and the knowledge to produce nuclear weapons...a threat to the very existence of all nations.

Committee for Economic Development
Nuclear Energy and National Security, **1976**

Where military spending is concerned, billions of dollars are treated like loose pocket change—$226 billion in the defense budget for fiscal 1982, more than double the entire GNP of India. To portray graphically how much a billion dollars is, a billion one-dollar bills placed end to end would stretch from here to the moon—and back!... The Administration's blueprint for military spending calls for a total of $1.3–$1.5 *trillion* over the next five years. To reach $1.5 trillion we would have to stack up 15 piles of $1000 bills, each pile as tall as Mt. Everest, the world's tallest mountain.

Professor Robert Lee
The Christian Century, **November 1981**

If one spent $1 million a day for 2000 years it would equal one-half of the Reagan Administration's proposed defense budget of 1.5 trillion for 1983 to 1988.

Anonymous

(Facts on military expenditures versus human needs can be found in Chapter 7—**Violence of Unused Weapons**—page 61.)

3
Mentality
of the Arms Race

* Someday science may have the existence of mankind in its power and the human race commit suicide by blowing up the world.

Henry Adams, 1862

We have now reached the age of unlimited power predicted nearly a century ago by Henry Adams: but we have neglected to heed his warning about the "effect of unlimited power on limited minds," and this farsighted anticipation of the madness of a nuclear arms race.

Sydney J. Harris
Detroit Free Press, **April 1984**

* The greatest danger is the danger created by inventing weapons capable of destroying civilization faster than we produce men who can be trusted to use them wisely.

George Bernard Shaw

* We have guided missiles and misguided men.

Martin Luther King

We have grasped the mystery of the atom and rejected the Sermon on the Mount. Ours is a world of nuclear giants and ethical infants. We know more about war than we do about peace—more about killing than we do about living.

General Omar Bradley

We have made a great advance in technology without a corresponding advance in moral sense. We are capable of unbinding the forces which lie at the heart of creation and of destroying our civilization.

Archbishop of Canterbury
Anglican (Episcopal) Church, 1981

I should like to invent a substance or a machine with such terrible power of mass destruction that war would thereby be made impossible for ever.

Alfred Nobel

Perhaps my dynamite plants will put an end to war sooner than your [peace] congresses. On the day two army corps can annihilate each other in one second all civilized nations will recoil from war in horror.

Alfred Nobel

Once a weapon has been developed...it will be used.

Kurt Waldheim
Secretary-General, United Nations

I voiced to [Secretary of War Stimson] my grave misgivings...on the basis of my belief that Japan was already defeated and dropping the bomb was completely unnecessary...as a measure to save American lives.

Dwight D. Eisenhower

It is my opinion that the use of this barbarous weapon at Hiroshima and Nagasaki was of no material assistance in our war against Japan. The Japanese were already defeated and ready to surrender because of the effective sea blockade and the successful bombing with conventional weapons.

It was my reaction that the scientists and others wanted to make this test because of the vast sums that had been spent on the project.... My own feeling is that in being the first to use it, we had adopted an ethical standard common to the barbarians of the dark ages. I was not taught to make war in that fashion, and wars cannot be won by destroying women and children.

Admiral William D. Leahy
Chief of Staff under F.D.R. and Harry Truman

I confess that I cannot understand how we can plot, lie, cheat and commit murder abroad and remain humane, honorable, trustworthy and trusted at home.

Archibald Cox

* A poet can write about a man slaying the dragon, but not about a man pushing a button that releases a bomb.

W. H. Auden

In the thirty-six years since the atomic bombings of Hiroshima and Nagasaki, a new language has evolved....Nukespeak is the language of nuclear development....atrocities are rendered invisible by sterile words like "megadeaths," nuclear war is called a "nuclear exchange." Nuclear weapons accidents are called "broken arrows" and "bent spears." Plutonium is called a "potential nuclear explosive." The accident at Three Mile Island was called an "event," an "incident"...and a "normal aberration."...India called its nuclear bomb a "peaceful nuclear device."

Nukespeak: The Selling of Nuclear Technology in America

The nuclear arms race has nothing to do with defense, little to do with deterrence, and everything to do with a monopoly of U.S. intervention in other countries while blocking Soviet intervention.

Randall Forsberg

...the arms race is a system based on faith...faith that human nature works in the way that deterrence theorists say it does, faith that deterrence itself should be credited with preventing war, and faith that if deterrence prevented war in one generation then it can prevent war in the next despite radically changed technological and political circumstances.

Richard J. Barnet

Deterrence is like the old story of the man who fell off the skyscraper and shouted, as he plummeted past the tenth floor, "I'm doing all right so far."

Ed Snyder
Executive Secretary
Friends Committee on National Legislation

Europe's reluctance to have medium-range missiles on its soil results more than anything else from a growing suspicion—reinforced by careless White House utterances—that the Reagan Administration regards those missiles not as instruments of deterrence but as instruments of war.

George W. Ball
former Undersecretary of State

United States policy under seven presidents has never renounced the first use of nuclear weapons.

Melvin Price
Chairperson
House Armed Services Committee

From Secretaries of Defense...

...our basic defense policy is based on the use of atomic weapons in a major war and is based on the use of such atomic weapons as would be militarily feasible and usable in a smaller war, if such a war is forced upon us.

Charles Wilson
Secretary of Defense
1958

It would be our policy to use nuclear weapons wherever we felt it necessary to protect our forces and achieve our objectives.

Robert McNamara
Secretary of Defense
1961

If there were any hint from the U.S. government that we were to accept the blandishments of a few people in the arms control community or a few people on Capitol Hill that we would refrain from first use, that would have a devastating effect on NATO because NATO depends, in large degree, psychologically as well as in terms of force structure, on nuclear reinforcement of conventional capabilities, should that be necessary.

James R. Schlesinger
Secretary of Defense
1975

The United States has never ruled out a first use of nuclear weapons. If an enemy, whether by stealth and deception or by large-scale mobilization, should attempt to defeat U.S. and allied conventional forces, it is NATO and U.S. policy to take whatever action is necessary to restore the situation.... Accordingly, to the extent that a nuclear response may be required locally, theater nuclear forces have an indispensable function to perform in defense and deterrence.

Donald Rumsfeld
Secretary of Defense
1977

It is essential that we maintain the capability at all times to inflict an unacceptable level of damage on the Soviet Union, including destruction of a minimum of 200 major Soviet cities.

Harold Brown
Secretary of Defense
1978

When it comes to strategic thermonuclear war, I don't think there is such a thing as a number one or number two. In exchanging strategic nuclear weapons, the damage to both parties would be so great that there is no winner, and therefore no such thing as number one and number two.

Harold Brown
Secretary of Defense
1978

I think we need to have a counterforce capability. Over and above that, I think that we need to have a war-fighting capability.

Frank Carlucci
Deputy Secretary of Defense
1981

If conventional means are insufficient to ensure a satisfactory termination of war, the U.S. will prepare options for the use of nuclear weapons.

Department of Defense Guidance
1982

No matter what their original intent may have been, I cannot believe that any atomic power would accept defeat while withholding its best weapon....So eventually, even though it starts out to be nonatomic war, war between atomic powers, it seems to me, will inevitably be atomic war.

Donald A. Quarles
Secretary of the Air Force

The first use of U.S. tactical nuclear weapons would probably be in a defensive mode based on prepared defense plans. Later use could include nuclear support for offensive operations to destroy the enemy or regain lost territory.

Department of the Army
Operations Field Manual 100-5
1976

I have no faith in the so-called controlled use of atomic weapons. There is no dependable distinction between tactical and strategic situations. I would not recommend the use of any atomic weapon, no matter how small, when both sides have the power to destroy the world.

Admiral Charles R. Brown

[Regarding limited nuclear war remaining limited]: You could have a pessimistic outlook on it or an optimistic. I always tend to be optimistic.

Ronald Reagan
Boston Globe
November 1981

The image of an American president carefully and calmly discussing over the Hotline the "limited" nature of an American nuclear attack in progress with the leaders of the Kremlin would be comical if it were not so tragic.

Jerry Elmer
American Friends Service Committee

The Administration's belief that it can control its forces throughout a prolonged nuclear war is naive at best, foolhardy and dangerous at worst.

Defense Monitor
1983

Limiting nuclear war is like limiting the mission of a match thrown in a keg of gunpowder.

John Culver
former Senator, Iowa

Europeans, of course, ask themselves, "limited to what?" and the answer is clear: limited to Europe.

Dorothee Sölle
German theologian

Any use of nuclear weapons would run the risk of rapid escalation...

Harold Brown
former Secretary of Defense

We [scientists] know with the certainty of established truth, that if enough of these weapons are made by enough different states, some of them are going to blow up—through accident or folly or madness.

C. P. Snow
English physicist

Modern history offers no example of the cultivation by rival powers of armed force on a massive scale which did not end in an outbreak of hostilities.

George Kennan
former US Ambassador to the USSR

Some have said that the Soviet Union has already achieved superiority over the US. The truth is that we are second to none. The impulse and the passion for military superiority must be seen for what they are: unrealistic, simplistic, dangerous.

Harold Brown
former Secretary of Defense

* What difference does it make whether someone's first or sixth or ninth if he can destroy another nation eight or ten times over? Whether you're first or second is irrelevant, isn't it? **Paul Newman**

The arms race is like two kids standing in a room full of gasoline up to their knees. Both are collecting matches and thinking that the more matches they collect, the more secure they will be. **Anonymous**

The nuclear arms race is the strangest military competition in history. Before the nuclear age a nation could calculate its killing power, measure it against that of its enemy, and make a rational judgement whether to go to war.... But such a judgment is impossible in the world of the atomic bomb because there is no objective that is worth the destruction of your own society, and the risks of such destruction in what modern-day strategists blandly call a "nuclear exchange" are very great.

Richard J. Barnet

When I think of the ever escalating nuclear arms race, I think of alcoholics, who know that liquor is deadly, and who, nevertheless, can always find one more reason for one more drink.

William Sloane Coffin

Even the term "arms race" is misleading. It implies that the side with the most weapons will be the winner.

Parents and Teachers for Social Responsibility

Whoever does not understand that the danger lies not in the possibility that someone else might have more missiles and warheads than we do, but in the very existence of these unconscionable quantities of highly poisonous explosives, and their existence, above all, in hands as weak and shaky and undependable as those of ourselves or our adversaries or any other mere human beings; whoever does not understand these things is never going to guide us out of this increasingly dark and menacing forest of bewilderment into which we have all wandered.

George Kennan
former US Ambassador to the USSR
Albert Einstein Peace Prize recipient
1981

For if reality is not something we can fully understand, and if we can make errors, we must be certain we are not carrying hydrogen bombs when we stumble and bump into unexpected events.

David McReynolds

The simplest meaning of the nuclear arms race is that the world's most powerful nations are prepared to commit mass murder.

Jim Wallis
Sojourners

...we are rapidly getting to the point that no war can be *won*. War implies a contest; when you get to the point that contest is no longer involved and the outlook comes close to destruction of the enemy and suicide for ourselves—an outlook that neither side can ignore—then arguments as to the exact amount of available strength as compared to somebody else's are no longer the vital issues.

Dwight D. Eisenhower
April 1956

In the past, war has been accepted as the ultimate arbiter of disputes among nations. But in the nuclear era we can no longer think of war as merely a continuation of diplomacy by other means. Nuclear war cannot be measured by the archaic standards of victory and defeat.

Jimmy Carter

The danger of nuclear war lies largely within us. It lies in how we think about winning, in how we define success, and in our illusions of being able to impose results.

Roger Fisher

In a nuclear war there are no winners or losers. It's not like conventional war where armies fight, one side wins, the other loses and everybody goes home. Nuclear war is a mutual unleashing of genocidal forces...

Dr. Robert Jay Lifton
Yale University Medical School

We are quite literally a nation which is in the process of committing suicide in the hope that then the Russians will not be able to murder it.

Dorothy Day

War has become a Frankenstein to destroy both sides. No longer does it possess the chance of the winner of the duel—it contains rather the germ of double suicide.

General Douglas MacArthur
July 1961

The war planning process of the past has become totally obsolete. Attack is now suicide.

Thomas J. Watson, Jr.
President, IBM

The most monumental, dangerous illusion of our time is the belief that any nation can win an all-out war.

John Culver
former Senator, Iowa

...it is contrary to reason to hold that war is now a suitable way to restore rights that have been violated.

Pope John XXIII

Nuclear war is not a solution. It is worse than any problem it might "solve."

Roger Fisher
Professor of Law, Harvard

* It's very difficult and somewhat embarrassing for military men to accept the fact that we have no defense against Soviet missiles and that the Soviets have no defense against our missiles. We can destroy the Soviet Union even though they destroy us first. There are no *winners* in a nuclear war.

Rear Admiral Gene R. La Rocque
U.S. Navy (retired)

* The guy in the street is the smart guy, he knows you can't fight and win a nuclear war. It's only the generals who are brought up to fight who think you can survive.

Dr. Herbert Scoville, Jr.
former Deputy Director for Research
CIA

...will the Soviet Union and the U.S. destroy civilization to ensure that their economic system and their political philosophy dominate the world? The answer is clear. Both the United States and the Soviet Union are planning, training, arming, and practicing to destroy each other and all civilization. Neither side expects to win. Neither side can avoid losing.

Rear Admiral Gene R. La Rocque
U.S. Navy (retired)
June 1983

Within a month [in 1969] I had met the first of a small but not uninfluential community of people who violently opposed SALT for a simple reason: It might keep America from developing a first-strike capability against the Soviet Union. I'll never forget being lectured by an Air Force colonel about how we should have "nuked" the Soviets in the late 1940s before they got The Bomb. I was told that if SALT would go away, we'd soon have the capability to nuke them again—and this time we'd use it.

Roger Molander
former nuclear strategist for
the White House's National Security Council
March 1982

Sometime later in this decade, military plans which are being seriously discussed now by the military establishments on both sides would lead to...an immediate exchange...in a nuclear war of something between 10,000 and 20,000 megatons each...

Dr. Bernard Feld
Professor, MIT

Depending on certain assumptions, some estimates predict 10 million casualties on one side and 100 million on the other. But that is not the whole population.

Eugene Rostow
former Chief U.S. Arms Negotiator

The dangers of atomic war are overrated. It would be hard on little concentrated countries like England. In the United States we have lots of space.

Colonel Robert Rutherford McCormick

With greatly increased offensive and defensive preparations the United States could hold casualties in a nuclear war to 20 million, a level compatible with survival and recovery.

Colin Gray
State Department Consultant

A nuclear war could alleviate some of the factors leading to today's ecological disturbances that are due to current high-population concentrations and heavy industrial production.

U.S. Office of Civil Defense Official

To plan for nuclear wars in which tens of millions would die is to say that crimes against humanity are justifiable in the interests of national security.

Wes Michaelson
Sojourners
February 1977

We are dragging heaven into hell. Our nation and the Soviet Union are turning the vast reach of space into a battlefield for new and terrifying machines of destruction.

Union of Concerned Scientists

We will be doing in space all that we are doing in the atmosphere, on the ground and at sea. We are preparing to wage wars and to win them.

Major General John H. Starrie
U.S. Air Force Director for Space Affairs
speech to a House committee, 1983

We need not strain our imagination to see that the nation controlling space will also be the one controlling the world.

Edward Aldridge
Pentagon Undersecretary

I clearly recognize that defensive systems have limitations and raise certain problems and ambiguities. If paired with offensive systems, they can be viewed as fostering an aggressive policy.

Ronald Reagan
March 1983

I don't know of any country that has gotten into war by being too strong, unless it was an aggressive nation.

Ronald Reagan

The President says he is absolutely convinced that "Star Wars" will work...despite the fact that hundreds of today's most brilliant scientists have condemned proposals for a space-based weapons system as "illusions," "fantasies," and "totally science fiction."

Union of Concerned Scientists

The atomic bomb is a marvelous gift that was given to us by a wise God.

Phyllis Schlafly

People who believe absurdities will commit atrocities.

Anonymous

In the real world of real political leaders—whether here or in the Soviet Union—a decision that would bring even one hydrogen bomb on one city of one's own country would be recognized in advance as a catastrophic blunder; ten bombs on ten cities would be a disaster beyond history; and a hundred bombs on one hundred cities are unthinkable.

McGeorge Bundy
Advisor to President Kennedy

Nothing in human history is more obscene than the cool discussions of competing nuclear strategies by apocalyptic game-players. All sorts of scenarios are being put forward about the circumstances under which we would drop bombs on the Soviet Union and the Soviet Union would drop bombs on us, as though both countries were involved in nothing more than a super backgammon game. The strategists in both countries need to be reminded that they are not playing with poker chips but with human lives and the whole of the human future.

Norman Cousins
Saturday Review
December 1981

The unfortunate situation is that today we are moving—sliding down hill—toward the probability or the likelihood that a nuclear conflict will actually break out—and that somebody will use one of these nuclear weapons in a conflict or perhaps even by accident.

Herbert Scoville, Jr.
former Deputy Director for Research, CIA

Missiles will bring anti-missiles, and anti-missiles will bring anti-anti-missiles. But inevitably, this whole electronic house of cards will reach a point where it can be constructed no higher.

General Omar Bradley
November 1957

* We have gone on piling weapon upon weapon, missile upon missile, new levels of destructiveness upon old ones, helplessly, almost involuntarily, like victims of some sort of hypnotism, like men in a dream, like lemmings heading for the sea.

George Kennan
former US Ambassador to the USSR

However useless a defense concept, an argument to proceed is deemed conclusive on one of two grounds. Either the Russians are doing it and therefore we must do it in order to avoid falling behind, or the Russians are not doing it and therefore we must in order to stay ahead.

Patricia Schroeder
Congressperson, Colorado

The strongest argument in behalf of massive military spending is that the other side is spending at least as much or more. No one stops to inquire whether the other side may be spending its money wisely or whether, indeed, our own spending has anything to do with genuine safety. It is almost as though we can preserve our "manhood" only by superior foolishness.

Norman Cousins

Why then do the superpowers persist in the arms race? The arms race has been self-propelling. Around the country thousands of scientists and engineers are developing weapons to counter weapons the Russians are expected to have eight to ten years from now. These people have a strong stake in continuing the arms race. So too have the Pentagon and the 22,000 prime contractors and 100,000 subcontractors who grow rich from military procurement. Others with an economic stake include the leadership of many unions whose members look to jobs from military production; academia which looks to research and development funds; the mayors and newspaper editors of cities who want defense contracts for investment in their areas; the "think tanks" that are paid large sums to devise a rationale for the arms race. Cementing together this military-industrial complex is the deliberately implanted thesis that "you cannot trust the Russians."

Sid Lens
"Launching the Arms Race"—*Mobilizer*, 1985

Defense contractors and their lobbyists argue that competition for defense business is an effective check on excessive profits.... But in fact there is little competition in defense work. Except for some common items such as food and clothing, most defense procurement is placed on a noncompetitive basis. Few firms can muster the financial, engineering, and manufacturing resources to perform multimillion-dollar defense contracts.... In fiscal year 1978 only about 8% of these contracts were awarded on a formally advertized, truly competitive basis.... The remaining 92% were either sole-source procurement or competitive-negotiated, where only a few firms can perform the work...

Admiral Hyman G. Rickover
March 1977

This conjunction of an immense military establishment and a large arms industry is new in the American experience.... We recognize the imperative need for this development. Yet we must not fail to comprehend its grave implications.... In the councils of government, we must guard against the acquisition of unwarranted influence, whether sought or unsought, by the military-industrial complex. The potential for the disastrous rise of misplaced power exists and will persist.

Dwight D. Eisenhower

We must admit that we are intoxicated with our science and technology (and) deeply committed to a Faustian bargain which is rapidly killing us spiritually and will soon kill us all physically.

Joseph Weizenbaum, MIT

You cannot simultaneously prevent and prepare for war.
Albert Einstein

There is an old Roman proverb that says: "If you would wish for peace, then prepare for war." *Rubbish!* If you would wish for peace, then offer alternatives to war!
Barbara Ward

The way to prevent war is to bend every energy towards preventing it, not to proceed by the dubious indirection of preparing for it.
Max Lerner

Arming in order to provide incentive to disarm has usually turned out to resemble growing obese in order to have incentive to diet and reduce. It only produces a fatter arsenal.
Clergy and Laity Concerned

It is quite strange, in fact, that as yet there is no such thing as a science of peace, since the science of war appears to be highly advanced....As a collective human phenomenon, however, even war involves a mystery, for all the people of the earth, who profess to be eager to banish war as the worst of scourges, are nonetheless the very ones who concur in the starting of wars and who willingly support armed combat.
Maria Montessori

* One of the most persistent ambiguities we face is that everybody talks about peace as a goal, but among the wielders of power peace is practically nobody's business. Many men cry "Peace! Peace!" but they refuse to do the things that make for peace.
The large power blocs talk passionately of pursuing peace while expanding defense budgets that already bulge, enlarging already awesome armies and devising ever more devastating weapons. Call the roll of those who sing the glad tidings of peace and one's ears will be surprised by the responding sounds. The heads of all nations issue clarion calls for peace, yet they come to the peace table accompanied by bands of brigands each bearing unsheathed swords.
Martin Luther King, Jr.
Where Do We Go from Here: Chaos or Community?

It is startling to realize that nuclear war is no longer "unthinkable." It is not uncommon for people today to imagine, fear, even expect war. Few people imagine, anticipate, and expect peace. It is not war but world peace that has become "unthinkable."
Waging Peace
Statement of Purpose

Peace, to many, has become a fighting word.   **Anonymous**

I don't think about it, there's nothing I can do about it.

Classic Nonsequitur

On a global scale, members of the human family are acting like many victims of domestic violence. They appear ready to passively accept their "beating," believing somehow that it is "deserved" or, in any case, that there is no way out.

Waging Peace
Statement of Purpose

My fellow Americans, I am pleased to tell you I just signed legislation which outlaws Russia forever. The bombing begins in five minutes.

Ronald Reagan
August 1984

I was wondering if people really know what war is. It's not like kids— they just fight. We could have a nuclear war and kill off the whole world; it's not just a fist fight.

Anonymous 6th Grader

* My suggestion is quite simple. Put the codes that are needed to fire nuclear weapons in a little capsule, and then implant that capsule right next to the heart of a volunteer. The volunteer would carry with him a big, heavy butcher knife as he accompanied the President. If ever the President wanted to fire nuclear weapons, the only way he could do so would be for him to first, with his own hands, kill one human being. The President says, "George, I'm sorry but tens of millions must die." He has to look at someone and realize what death is—what an innocent death is. Blood on the White House carpet. It's really brought home.

When I suggested this to friends in the Pentagon they said, "My God, that's terrible. Having to kill someone would distort the President's judgement. He might never push the button."

Roger Fisher
co-founder, Harvard Negotiation Project
Evolutionary Blues

A nuclear explosion is many times more powerful than a TNT explosion, and you shouldn't have much trouble recognizing one…. Count the number of seconds between the flash of light and the bang (explosion). If you are in charge or alone, submit this information as an NBC 1 report. Stay calm, check for injury, check your weapon and equipment for damage, check your buddies, and get ready to go on with your mission.

U.S. Army Field Manual
FM 21-41

Dig a hole, cover it with a couple of doors, and then throw three feet of dirt on top. It's the dirt that does it…. Everybody's going to make it if there are enough shovels to go around. Dirt is the thing that protects you from the blast and the radiation—Dirt is just great stuff.

T. K. Jones
Deputy Undersecretary of Defense for Strategic Nuclear Forces
January 1982

Following a nuclear attack on the United States, the U.S. Postal Service plans to distribute Emergency Change of Address Cards.

Executive Order 11490
Federal Emergency Management Agency
1969

You will be allowed three pounds of meat, six eggs, seven pints of milk, four pounds of cereal, and one-half pound of fats and oils per week.

Executive Order 11490
FEMA
1969

Be sure to carry your credit cards, cash, checks, stocks, insurance policies, and will. Every effort will be made to clear trans– nuclear attack checks, including those drawn on destroyed banks. You will be encouraged to buy U.S. Savings Bonds.

Executive Order 11490
FEMA
1969

If the attack happens on July 1, say some people have paid withholding and some people have paid nothing, but you have to forgive and forget on both sides.

Executive Order 11490
FEMA
1969

Dear Mr. President,
    Please tell me how I can be a leader. I heard you are going to save the leaders in the nuclear war. Me and my dog want to be leaders.

Love,
Lisa
P.S. Please make Amy and her dog leaders too.

If we reach, or when we reach, Heaven's scenes, we truly will find it guarded by United States Marines.

Ronald Reagan
June 1985
from the Marine Corps Hymn

...many...have grown tired of just watching as the leaders of the superpowers behave like teenagers playing chicken on the highway to catastrophe.

Ellen Goodman
The Boston Globe
November 1981

...we will no longer be led only by that half of the population whose socialization, through toys, games, values, and expectations, sanctions violence as the final assertion of manhood, synonymous with nationhood.

Wilma Scott Heide

* Every man will fall who, born a man, proudly presumes to be a superman.

Sophocles

[Speaking of males] Of course his attempt to make himself Lord has kept him, in fact, a child.

Barbara Deming
Love Has Been Exploited Labor

Out of our posturing and game-playing comes the growing and dangerous tendency to think of nuclear weapons as political symbols, as message bearers. But we cannot count on them remaining just political symbols. They're becoming all the more deadly and more vulnerable. And that increases the risk that a nuclear war will start out of panic. There is an easier way to send a message—and that is through communication.

Paul Warnke
Chief SALT II Negotiator

Project ELF is not communication. Communication is meeting people, talking with people, working for peace.

Women's Peace Presence

* We profess that we in the "free world" put a special value upon men's lives. This is supposedly precisely what differentiates us from our antagonists. It is in the name of this difference, in fact, that—by a queer logic—we profess our willingness to risk the continued existence of mankind.

Barbara Deming

[National interest] involves making the Soviets an offer for the sake of our nation which they find too attractive to refuse. [National advantage] involves making the Soviets an offer they cannot accept in order to keep or attain an advantage which we desire.

Wisconsin Clergy and Laity Concerned
Newsletter
August 1984

A phenomenon noticeable throughout history regardless of place or period is the pursuit of governments of policies contrary to their own interest.

Barbara W. Tuchman
The March of Folly

"In God We Trust." That is on our coins. We in America pretend to believe that. We do not. We trust only in weapons and bribes and treaties and admonitions—as does our adversary. The old, old history—the history of death.

Taylor Caldwell
The Listener

ADDITIONS:

4
Insanity of Warmaking

We are healthy only to the extent that our ideas are humane.

Kurt Vonnegut, Jr.

* A psychiatrist found Eichmann "perfectly sane".... Sanity is no longer a value or an end itself. The "sanity" of modern man is about as useful to him as the huge bulk and muscles of the dinosaur. If he were a little less sane, a little more doubtful, a little more aware of his absurdities and contradictions, perhaps there might be a possibility of survival.

Thomas Merton

* War has always seemed to me "the ultimate insanity." Violence and war as the maximum demonstration of man's capacity for inhumanity to man were against my religious beliefs, my sense of morality, and my common sense.

Dag Hammarskjöld

* Have you ever thought that war is a madhouse and that everyone in the war is a patient? Tell me, how can a normal man get up in the morning knowing that in an hour or a minute he may no longer be there? How can he walk through heaps of decomposing corpses and then sit down at the table and calmly eat a roll? How can he defy nightmare-risks and then be ashamed of panicking for a moment?

Oriana Fallaci
Nothing and *So Be It*

We have to have armies! We have to have military power! We have to have police forces, whether it's police in a great city or police in an international scale to keep those madmen from taking over the world and robbing the world of its liberties.

Billy Graham
1965

The people of the United States want peace. The people of China want peace. The people of the Soviet Union want peace. Why can't we have peace? We don't realize the proliferation of these weapons and the arms race of $400 billion that we're spending on arms in the world—insanity, madness!

Billy Graham, 1979

Soldiers with fingers on nuclear triggers are regularly tested for "sanity." Sanity in this case is defined as willingness to calmly obey orders. These orders might include the destruction of cities.

Anonymous

Thus the greatest anomaly of all in our time is the imitation of madness. Society has devised a phrase that stifles the moral indignation, paralyzes the rational intelligence, and produces unreasoning acquiescence. The phrase is "national security." It is not necessary for those who invoke this magical phrase to demonstrate exactly how the national security will be served by any of the cataclysmic terrors that now inhabit the arsenals. All that is necessary is to point to the Russians. And, in this world of mirror images, all that is necessary for the Russians is to point to the Americans. The madness is reciprocal, inexorable, inexcusable.

Norman Cousins

The dynamic of the arms race is the manufacture of fear. In the name of shoring up deterrence, proponents of the arms race on one side fuel the fears of those on the other, and then on it goes in a self-perpetuating spiral. The peace movement's target has to be the arms-racers' symbiotic paranoia.

Todd Gitlin

* The arms race is a race with one's own shadow. No matter how fast you go, the other guy's going to keep up with you and stay connected with you; in fact, he's a part of you. He is the projection of yourself—of your dark side. No one will win the arms race, nor will anyone drop out. We can never out-distance the fear of those parts of ourselves that we have projected on others: Americans on Russians, Jews on Arabs, Protestants on Catholics, whites on blacks. Making the bomb the issue and disarmament the goal shields us only briefly from the realization that it is we ourselves—we human beings—that are the source of the danger. We must understand why we are afraid of our "shadow." What is the origin of the fear of the "other," and how can we deal with it? Why do we project on other societies qualities we have within ourselves, and then maintain that they are bad guys and we are the good? They are, of course, doing the same thing with us.

Robert Fuller

If American nuclear power is to support U.S. foreign policy objectives, the United States must possess the ability to wage nuclear war rationally.

Colin S. Gray and Keith Payne
Victory is Possible

We are dealing here with nothing less than the logic of madness...
Robert Jay Lifton and Richard Falk
Indefensible Weapons

This entire preoccupation with nuclear war, which appears to hold most of our government in its grasp, is a form of illness.

George Kennan
former US Ambassador to the USSR

It can be taken as an axiom that if the human race is mad enough to construct the means of its own destruction, it contains within itself the madness to use those means.

David McReynolds

To try to win a war, to set victory as an aim, is pure madness, since total war with nuclear weapons will be fatal to both sides.

B. H. Liddell Hart
Defense or Deterrence, **1962**

We prepare for our extinction in order to insure our survival...

Jonathan Schell
The Fate of the Earth

Shelters are fine except for three things: getting to them, staying in them, and getting out of them. It's a dangerous illusion to tell the American public that shelters will protect them.

Robert Jay Lifton
Professor, Yale University

[Regarding civil defense preparations for nuclear war] When such a fantasy structure becomes fixed, we call it a delusion. This fantasy or delusion is a product not of individual but of social madness. We thus encounter the kind of situation in which individual people who are psychologically "normal" (in the sense of being functional in a given society) can collude in forms of thought structure that are unreal in the extreme...

Robert Jay Lifton
Richard Falk
Indefensible Weapons

The Supreme Trick of mass insanity is that it persuades you that the only abnormal person is the one who refuses to join in the madness of others, the one who tries vainly to resist.   **Eugène Ionesco**

The unseen madness is to live life as usual under the threat of nuclear holocaust.   **Interhelp**

But there are some things in our social system to which all of us ought to be maladjusted....I never intend to become adjusted to the madness of militarism and the self-defeating method of physical violence.

Martin Luther King, Jr.

...to be unemotional about the end of the earth approaching, is mentally sick. To feel no feelings about it, to be uninvolved is inappropriate, to be psychologically comfortable today, absolutely inappropriate.

Dr. Helen Caldicott
Physicians for Social Responsibility

Lack of emotionalism in discussions about nuclear war is not a sign of reason, but of a sick passivity.

Alice Cook
British Journalist

...the worst insanity is to be totally without anxiety, totally sane.

Thomas Merton

When life itself seems lunatic, who knows where madness lies?...To surrender dreams...this may be madness....Too much sanity may be madness and, the maddest of all, to see life as it is and not as it should be.

Don Quixote in
Man of La Mancha

Where does one go from a world of insanity? Somewhere on the other side of despair.

T. S. Eliot

ADDITIONS:

ADDITIONS:

5
Insecurity of
Nuclear Weapons

As our military strength approaches infinity, our security approaches zero.

Speak Truth to Power
American Friends Service Committee

Our security is the total product of our economic, intellectual, moral, and military strengths.... There is no way in which a country can satisfy the craving for absolute security—but it can easily bankrupt itself, morally and economically, in attempting to reach that illusory goal through arms alone.

Dwight D. Eisenhower

The weakness of the United States is not caused by insufficient arms but by insufficient wisdom. Our judgements are out of balance and out of touch with reality. They lack a feeling for history and principle. They have been angry, impulsive, and irrational—unguided by any sound policy. Its military spending is indiscriminate. It buys fat as well as muscle—insecurity as well as security.

Adlai Stevenson
former Senator, Illinois

Reliance on weapons and brute force for strength has come to a dead end. The road to peace via competition for military superiority has not led to safety but to greater insecurity and danger.

Women's Peace Presence

The biggest threat to our security is the arms race itself.

I. F. Stone

Grownups can't be trusted with guns and bombs.

Cynthia G.
Milwaukee
Age 8
Please Save My World

* ...I doubt that any columnist...is concerning himself with what is the true security problem of the day. That problem is not merely man against man or nation against nation. It is man against war.

Dwight D. Eisenhower
April 1956

There are powerful voices around the world who still give credence to the old Roman concept—if you desire peace, prepare for war. This is absolute nuclear nonsense and I repeat—it is a disastrous misconception to believe that by increasing the total uncertainty one increases one's own certainty.

Lord Mountbatten
August 1979

As a military man who has given half a century of active service I say in all sincerity that the nuclear arms race has no military purpose. Wars cannot be fought with nuclear weapons. Their existence only adds to our perils because of the illusions which they have generated.

Lord Mountbatten
August 1979

The human tragedy reaches its climax in the fact that after all the exertions and sacrifices of hundreds of millions of people...we have still not found peace or security and that we lie in the grip of even worse perils than those we have surmounted.

Winston Churchill

Today there is a growing awareness that the long reliance on violence has now produced a real danger of human extinction.

Anonymous

You do need one thing, security of life. Life is the greatest truth. And now you are being told, "If we build huge nukes, an arsenal and the whole thing, then we will have security." You will have only one security; you will be evaporated. We don't need that.

Yogi Bhajan

There is no presumption more terrifying than that of those who would blow up the world on the basis of their personal judgement of a transient situation.

George F. Kennan
former US Ambassador to the USSR

What's most frightening, however, is that we have not matured beyond this mindless historical game. And we now play this ancient game with what may be the world's last weapon, the ultimate silencer.

Rusty Schweickart
Apollo astronaut

It gets harder for any of us to rest comfortably on a king-sized bed of missiles.

Ellen Goodman
The Boston Globe, **November 1981**

The term "national security" has a built-in contradiction: in the atomic age, no *national* security is possible. Either we have a workable world security system or we have nothing. The efforts of the individual nations to achieve military supremacy or even adequacy are actually competitive and provocative in their effect.

Norman Cousins

We cannot make our end of the boat safer by making the Soviet end more likely to capsize. We cannot improve our security by making nuclear war more likely for them.

Roger Fisher

The global balance of terror, pioneered by the United States and the Soviet Union, holds hostage the citizens of the Earth.

Carl Sagan
Cosmos

Even though the "balance of terror" has been able to avoid the worst and may do so for some time more, to think that the arms race can thus go on indefinitely, without causing a catastrophe, would be a tragic illusion.

Pope Paul VI

...the security of the global community cannot forever rest on a balance of terror.

Jimmy Carter

The worst to be feared and the best to be expected can be simply stated. The *worst* is atomic war. The *best* would be this: a life of perpetual tension; a burden of arms draining the wealth and labor of all peoples; a wasting of strength that defies the American system or the Soviet system or any system to achieve true abundance of happiness for the peoples of this earth.

Dwight D. Eisenhower

Security as the good of a nation is incompatible with the insecurity of the people.

Brazilian Bishops
Christian Exigencies of a Political Order, 37
February 1977

I'm not really sure who is ahead in the arms race and I don't think it really matters. I mean, it doesn't make me happy to think that we're ahead, or sad to think that maybe the Russians are ahead. We both have enough bombs to kill each other, and if someone drops the bomb, no matter who, we all suffer. I would only feel secure if the U.S. got rid of its nuclear bombs.

Debra Britt
Age 15
Our Future at Stake

Dear Astronaut,
    Please take the nuclear bombs to the moon on your next space flight and leave them there.

Your friend,
Rachel L.
Chicago, Age 9
Please Save My World

In a nuclear war, the best defense is not to have an offense.

David Hoffman

This poses a terrible problem, because we at that point, particularly with the MX, would have a clear first-strike capability against their ICBMs, which would be devastating to them. They would have to consider a U.S. first strike whether we think we would do that or not.

General Lew Allen
US Air Force Chief of Staff
Senate Appropriations Committee Hearing
May 1981

From a security point of view we would be in a more dangerous position if both countries had systems which could threaten the other's ICBMs than if the Soviets alone had them. Having a missile which can threaten a major part of the Soviet deterrent is only asking the Soviets to launch a pre-emptive strike or put its missiles on launch on warning.

Herbert Scoville, Jr.
former CIA Deputy Director for Research
March 1982

Every government defends its participation in the arms race as necessary to guard its national security. But this is an illusion. What makes the arms race a global folly is that all countries are now buying greater and greater insecurity at higher and higher costs.

Alva Myrdal
Nobel Peace Prize Winner

The belief that it is possible to achieve security through armaments on a national scale is a disastrous illusion—in the last analysis the peaceful coexistence of peoples is primarily dependent upon mutual trust.

Albert Einstein

One of the questions which we have to ask ourselves as a country is— what in the name of God is strategic superiority? What is the significance of it—politically, militarily, operationally—at these levels of numbers? What do we do with it?

Henry Kissinger
1974

Nuclear superiority does no good.

I. F. Stone

Nuclear superiority is unattainable.

Paul Warnke
former chief SALT II negotiator
October 1980

Neither Communism nor anti-Communism can be built on mountains of human corpses.

Bertrand Russell

Fear at either end of the rifle only tends to pull the trigger.

Ned Richards
Courage in Both Hands

Only when we have alternatives to violence and the threat of violence for settling conflicts will we be truly secure.

Women's Peace Presence

ADDITIONS:

6
Consequences
of Nuclear War

We turned the switch, we saw the flashes, we watched them for about ten minutes—and then we switched everything off and went home. That night I knew that the world was headed for sorrow.

Leo Szilard
experimenting with nuclear fission
March 1939

If I knew then what I know now, I never would have helped to develop the bomb.

George Kistiakowsky
Manhattan Project scientist

In some sort of crude sense which no vulgarity, no humor, no overstatement can quite extinguish, the physicists have known sin; and this is a knowledge which they cannot lose.

J. Robert Oppenheimer
head of Manhattan Project

Updrafts became so violent that sheets of zinc roofing were hurled aloft....Disposing of the dead was a minor problem, but to clean the rooms and corridors of urine, feces, and vomit was impossible....The sight of them was most unbearable. Their faces and hands were burnt and swollen...their flesh was wet and mushy...their ears had melted off....I saw fire reservoirs filled to the brim with dead people who looked as though they had been burned alive...none of the patients had any appetite and were dying so fast I had begun to accept death as a matter of course...bloody diarrhea was increasing...sanitation teams were cremating the remains of people who had been killed. Looking out, I could discern numerous fires about the city....White chips of blistered paint and mortar settled over us like falling cherry blossoms....What a dismal view...the shabby figure of a dog trudging along with his hips bent, tail down, and hair gone.

Dr. Michihiko Hachiya
Hiroshima Diary

When I arrived, some were still alive. They were unable to move their bodies. The strongest were so weak that they were slumped over on the ground. I talked with them and they thought they would be O.K., but all of them would die within a week. I cannot forget the way their eyes looked at me and their voices spoke to me, forever.

Michito Ichimaru

...regaining consciousness, I found myself lying on the ground covered with pieces of wood. When I stood up in a frantic effort to look around, there was darkness. Terribly frightened, I thought I was alone in a world of death, and groped for any light.

Haruko Ogasawara

When the darkness began to fade, I found that there was nothing around me. My house, the next door neighbor's house, and the next had all vanished. I was standing amid the ruins of my house. No one was around. It was quiet, very quiet.

Haruko Ogasawara

* The bomb that fell on Hiroshima fell on America, too.
It fell on no city, no munition plants, no docks.
It erased no church, vaporized no public buildings,
    reduced no man to his atomic elements.
But it fell, it fell.
It burst. It shook the land.
God have mercy on our children.
God have mercy on America.

Hermann Hagerdorn
The Bomb That Fell on America

I'm not proud of the part I've played in it [the development of nuclear power]. That's why I'm such a strong proponent of stopping this whole nonsense of war. The lesson of history is that when a war starts, every nation will ultimately use whatever weapon has been available....we must expect that if another war...breaks out, we will use nuclear energy in some form. That's due to the imperfection of human beings....I think we'll probably destroy ourselves.

Admiral Hyman Rickover
January 1982

...if the inventory of East-West nuclear warheads and delivery systems were used in war it would kill hundreds of millions of persons, carry radioactive injury and death to many of the world's nations, profoundly damage the environment of the earth we live and depend on, and unhinge and devastate the target nations so effectively that they would no longer function as modern industrial states.

Union of Concerned Scientists

Immediate deaths—20–160 million.
Middle-term effects—Enormous economic destruction and disruption. If immediate deaths are in low range, more tens of millions may die subsequently because economy is unable to support them. Major question about whether economic viability can be restored. Unpredictable psychological effects.
Long-term effects—Cancer deaths and genetic damage in the millions; relatively insignificant in attacked areas, but quite significant elsewhere in the world.

Office of Technology Assessment
U.S. Congress
The Effects of Nuclear War

Neither they, nor we, could survive a thermonuclear war; that's the nature of a thermonuclear war, that devastation is so great that even good defenses don't suffice.

Harold Brown
Secretary of Defense
1977

I think that one is talking, when one talks about a full thermonuclear exchange, about damage to both countries so great that afterwards it would be hard to tell what recovery meant.

Harold Brown

...a war which, though regarded as a "limited war" by the superpowers, would be no less than a war of annihilation for the countries of the battlefield.

Helmut Schmidt
Chancellor of West Germany

Those leaders who speak of "winning" or surviving limited nuclear war can't be aware of the medical facts.

Dr. Howard Hiatt
Dean, Harvard School of Public Health

People are getting toughened about death. They do not realize the prolonged suffering of nuclear attacks, with hundreds of people taking weeks to die, screaming to be shot, with no medical help available. Our whole concept of a civilized response to a tragedy is totally inapplicable.

D. Thomas Chalmers
Mount Sinai Medical School
March 1981

If nuclear war begins, there will be no hospitals, no doctors, nothing to eat, no government. This will be the peace, the complete peace of the graveyard.

Shri R. S. Mishra, M.D.

Currently, U.S. defense preparedness planning expects some 40 to 60 million prompt fatalities after a nuclear explosion....It's not without interest that 20 years ago when a committee organized by the President studied the problem of providing health care in the post-attack era, their recommendation simply was to stock-pile opium to make it a little easier for people to get over into the other world. That still is our primary response to a nuclear attack—our opium and morphine stockpiles.

William Kincade

* It is my belief that any physician who even takes part in so-called emergency medical disaster planning—specifically to meet the problem of nuclear attack—is committing a profoundly unethical act. He is

deluding himself or herself, colleagues, and by implication the public at large, into the false belief that mechanisms of survival in any meaningful social sense are possible.

D. H. Jack Geiger
Physicians for Social Responsibility

Nuclear war would be the last epidemic our civilization would ever know.

Dr. Howard Hiatt
Dean, Harvard School of Public Health

War must be dealt with as an untreatable epidemic for which there is only one approach—that of prevention.

Dr. Howard Hiatt
Dean, Harvard School of Public Health

Scientists initially underestimated the effects of fall-out, were amazed that nuclear explosions in space disabled distant satellites, had no idea that the fireballs from high-yield thermonuclear explosions could deplete the ozone layer and missed altogether the possible climatic effects of nuclear dust and smoke.

Carl Sagan
The Nuclear Winter

Our results have been carefully scrutinized by more than 100 scientists in the United States, Europe, and the Soviet Union...the overall conclusion seems to be agreed upon: there are severe and previously unanticipated global consequences of nuclear war—sub-freezing temperatures in a twilit radioactive gloom lasting for months or longer.

Carl Sagan
The Nuclear Winter

Vast numbers of surviving humans would starve to death. The delicate ecological relations that bind together organisms on Earth in a fabric of mutual dependency would be torn, perhaps irreparably. There is little question that our global civilization would be destroyed. The human population would be reduced to prehistoric levels, or less. Life for any survivors would be extremely hard. And there seems to be a real possibility of the extinction of the human species.

...the heating of the vast quantities of atmospheric dust and soot in northern latitudes will transport these fine particles towards and across the Equator. The Southern Hemisphere would experience effects that, while less severe than in the Northern Hemisphere, are nevertheless extremely ominous. The illusion with which some people in the Northern Hemisphere reassure themselves—catching an Air New Zealand flight in a time of serious international crisis, or the like—is now much less tenable, even on the narrow issue of personal survival for those with the price of a ticket.

Carl Sagan
The Nuclear Winter

But what if nuclear war can be contained, and much less than 5000 megatons is detonated? Perhaps the greatest surprise in our work was that even small nuclear wars can have devastating climatic effects. We considered a war in which a mere 100 megatons were exploded, less than one percent of the world arsenals, and only in low-yield airbursts over cities. This scenario, we found, would ignite thousands of fires, and the smoke from these fires alone would be enough to generate an epoch of cold and dark almost as severe as in the 5000 megaton case. The threshold for what Richard Turco has called the Nuclear Winter is very low.

Carl Sagan
The Nuclear Winter

[I speak]...as one who has witnessed the horror and the lingering sadness of war—as one who knows that another war could utterly destroy this civilization which has been so slowly and painfully built over thousands of years.

Dwight D. Eisenhower

A nuclear Holocaust would silence life on our planet forever. It would not only be the death of human life and plants, but the death of music and painting and books. The silence is total and eternal. The earth only a rock spinning forever alone. It would be the death of life and the death of death itself.

Jonathan Schell and Helen Caldicott

The Stone Age may return on the gleaming wings of science.

Winston Churchill

ADDITIONS:

7
Violence of Unused Weapons

A.   Economic Implications

B.   Health and Environmental Effects

C.   Spiritual and Psychological Distress

Nuclear weapons in existence at this time have the potential to destroy life on this planet. In addition, these weapons kill without being used. The radiation-related diseases of uranium miners, the consumption of valuable natural resources, and the elimination of vital services for the poor and needy are aspects of the present effects of these murderous devices.

An Open Letter on the Nuclear Arms Race
from the Presbyterian Peace Fellowship, 1981

This world in arms is not spending money alone. It is spending the sweat of its laborers, the genius of its scientists, the hopes of its children.

Dwight D. Eisenhower
April 1953

A. Economic Implications

Were the money which it has cost to gain, at the close of a long war, a little territory...expended in improving what they already possess, in making roads, opening rivers, building ports, improving the arts and finding employment for the idle poor, it would render them [the nations] much stronger, healthier and happier. This I hope will be our wisdom.

Thomas Jefferson

It cost $200,000 to kill a single enemy in World War II, $500,000 per kill in Vietnam.

Franklin Pollard

It is a tragic mixup when the United States spends $500,000 for every enemy soldier killed, and only $53 annually on the victims of poverty.

Martin Luther King, Jr.
October 1967

Rockets and armies are poised to destroy the work of human hands and the creation of God, while each day warless violence kills by hunger and the withholding of necessities.

International Fellowship of Reconciliation

Every gun that is made, every warship launched, every rocket fired signifies, in the final sense, a theft from those who hunger and are not fed, those who are cold and are not clothed.

Dwight D. Eisenhower
April 1953

The arms race is one of the greatest curses on the human race; it is to be condemned as a danger, an act of aggression against the poor, and a folly which does not provide the security it promises.

Vatican Statement to the United Nations, 1976

In the long run, no country can advance intellectually and in terms of its culture and well-being if it has to devote everything to military buildup. I do not see much hope for a world engaged in this all-out effort on military buildup, military technology, and tremendous attempts at secrecy.

Dwight D. Eisenhower

A process of technical, industrial, and human deterioration has been set in motion within American society. The competence of the industrial system is being eroded at its base. Entire industries are falling into technical disrepair and there is a massive loss of productive employment because of inability to hold even domestic markets against foreign competition....The same basic depletion operates as an unseen hand restricting America's relations with the rest of the world, limiting foreign policy moves primarily to military-based initiatives. This deterioration is the result of an unprecedented concentration of America's technical talent and fresh capital on military production.

Seymour Melman
Our Depleted Society

* The old imperialism—exploitation of raw materials and of colonies—has been replaced by a new kind of imperialism: the pentagonist mother country exploits her own people in order to insure the aims of an economy permanently geared to war. The people are exploited as a source of labor and of taxes, which in turn assure that men and war material will be wasted in an endless cycle which profits only the military-industrial complex.

Dr. Juan Bosch
Pentagonism...a Substitute for Imperialism

The only solution to the current balance of terror is for the USA and the Soviet Union to wind down the arms race together....Military spending is by far the largest single expenditure from the federal government's general tax revenues and the largest contribution to the federal debt....Yet, this inflationary spending creates fewer jobs than the federal spending in the civilian economy.

William Winpisinger
President, International Association
of Machinists and Aerospace Workers
1979

World military expenditure equals the entire collective income of the poorest half of the world's population.

Housmans Peace Diary 1985

Developing countries are encouraged to spend five times as much money on importing arms as on buying agricultural equipment.

Housmans Peace Diary 1985

While so many people are going hungry, while so many families are suffering destitution, while so many people spend their lives submerged in the darkness of ignorance, while so many schools, hospitals, homes worthy of the name, are needed, every public or private squandering...every financially depleting arms race...all these we say become a scandalous and intolerable crime. The most serious obligation enjoined on us demands that we openly denounce it.

Pope Paul VI

Our weapons are our greatest danger. The superpowers hold 10 to 12 tons of TNT equivalent for every man, woman and child on the face of the earth. We are not only endangered from without, but from within—as the size of the Pentagon budget determines what is left for our human needs.

Ron Dellums
Representative, California

The arms race can kill, though the weapons themselves may never be used....by their cost alone, armaments kill the poor by causing them to starve.

Vatican Statement to the United Nations, 1976

Unused weapons are no less murderous—these require human energy and resources which are therefore not available to relieve desperate human needs. While a million dollars a minute is spent on the arms race, millions of people suffer malnutrition.

International Fellowship of Reconciliation

Today there is more tonnage of explosives in the world than tonnage of food.

Anonymous

Thirty children a minute are dying from hunger. If 10% of the world's military budget was converted to meet the needs of the hungry in the world, hunger could be obliterated.

World Bank

Today, about 27,000 people died from starvation and malnutrition-related diseases. Starvation could have been prevented for only 50 cents per person per day, or $13,500.
Today, the world spent over $2.2 billion on military expenditures.

Hunger Action Coalition

The money required to provide adequate food, water, education, health and housing for everyone in the world has been estimated at $17 billion a year. It is a huge sum of money...about as much as the world spends on arms every two weeks.

Anonymous

Today the United States and Russia have enough nuclear weapons to kill each person in the world 12 times.

Before we decide that we should cut back on health research in order to add to the nuclear overkill, I would ask you to do one thing. *Tomorrow at breakfast, take a look across the table* and ask yourself whether the security of the person you see is going to be more enhanced over the next 10 years by better heart research, better cancer research, better arthritis research or by an extra MX missile.

David Obey
Representative, Wisconsin
April 1986

The federal government is paying more attention to housing missiles than providing housing for people...

Richard Hatcher
Mayor of Gary, Indiana

Two-thirds of all governments spend more to guard their populations against military attack than against all the enemies of good health, while according to some estimates 70% of people die from preventable diseases.

Housmans Peace Diary 1985

Redirecting seven hours' worth of world military expenditure could eradicate malaria from the face of the world.

Housmans Peace Diary 1985

The cost of a single new nuclear submarine is the equivalent of total education spending in 23 low-income countries with 160 million school-age children.

Housmans Peace Diary 1985

We plan to build about 226 missiles at about $110,000,000 each. For each missile we cancel, we could eliminate poverty in 101,000 female-headed families for a year. If we cancelled the whole program, we could eliminate poverty for all children in the United States twice over and have enough left to send all female heads of low-income families to college for a year.

Marian Wright Edelman
President, Children's Defense Fund

The world spends eight times as much money developing new weapons as on researching new energy sources.

Housmans Peace Diary 1985

In an oil-short world, new tanks consume 1.9 gallons of petrol [gasoline] each mile.

Housmans Peace Diary 1985

Global arms spending is 2400 times higher than expenditures on international peacekeeping.

Housmans Peace Diary 1985

B. Health and Environmental Effects

Thousands of Americans have already been killed by nuclear weapons—our own.

from *Radiation: The Human Cost*
SANE

...[there are] estimates that up to two million Americans were present at [atomic bomb] tests potentially exposing them to some degree of low level radiation.

Malcolm W. Browne

The evidence mounts that, within the range of exposure levels encountered by radiation workers, there is no threshold, i.e., a level which can be assumed as safe in an absolute sense...any amount of radiation has a finite probability of inducing a health effect, e.g., cancer.

Robert Minoque and Karl Goller
Nuclear Regulatory Commission
September 1978

Nuclear fission is the most profound and dangerous tinkering ever introduced into the environment by human beings. Nuclear fission represents an incredible, incomparable and unique hazard for human life. People whose business it is to judge hazards, the insurance companies, refuse to insure nuclear power stations anywhere in the world.

E. F. Schumacher
Small Is Beautiful

From uranium mining to waste disposal, nuclear technology is at war with life.

Waging Peace

The problem faced by the atomic industry and the Federal government is simple to state: they have got millions of tons of deadly radioactive waste that has been accumulating for over 40 years, with no known safe way to dispose of it. Worse, the pile of waste is growing at an increasing pace because new uranium mines are opening, new nuclear power plants are being built, and more nuclear weapons are being produced.

Anonymous

* Whole empires have risen and fallen in a fraction of the time that Strontium and Cesium will have to remain sealed away. Neanderthal man appeared only about 75,000 years ago compared to the 250,000 years Plutonium needs to be guarded.

Friends for a Nonviolent World
Twin Cities Northern Sun Alliance
Want Not, Waste Not

* No degree of prosperity could justify the accumulation of large amounts of highly toxic substances which nobody knows how to make "safe" and which remain an incalculable danger to the whole of creation for historical or even geological ages. To do such a thing is a transgression against life itself.... It means conducting the economic affairs of man as if people (and creation) really did not matter at all.

E. F. Schumacher

Radioactive waste becomes a threat only if it escapes into the bio-system.

Nuclear waste is buried in eleven major sites in trenches that government officials assured us would contain the wastes safely for hundreds of years. In less than 10 years, 6 of them leaked.

Friends for a Nonviolent World
Twin Cities Northern Sun Alliance
Want Not, Waste Not

Testimony given at U.S. Department of Energy hearing on siting of a national high-level nuclear waste repository:

I don't care where they build it, it is too close to our children.
woman elder of Menominee (anonymous)

I will not have my son used in an experiment.
father of a 4-month-old son (anonymous)

If I had a patient who was in the process of creating a virtually permanent toxin, and who admitted this toxin could really not be contained or stored, but wanted to go ahead and make lots of this toxin anyway, I would have that person hospitalized and treated for obvious suicidal ideation.
Neil Nathan, M.D.

My grandmother told me to tell you that we could go indefinitely without nuclear power; we could go only about a week without water.

Anonymous

As a physician, I contend that nuclear technology threatens life on our planet with extinction. If present trends continue, the air we breathe, the food we eat, and the water we drink will soon be contaminated with enough radioactive pollutants to pose a potential health hazard far greater than any plague humanity has ever experienced.

Dr. Helen Caldicott
Physicians for Social Responsibility

For me this [the nuclear freeze] is a family issue and a medical issue. I took the Hippocratic Oath of healing seriously and the nuclear freeze is the ultimate medical issue.

Dr. Helen Caldicott
November 1983

Our nuclear program was built in the name of national security— protecting the lives of Americans. One can't help but wonder, who was protected and at whose expense?

Pat Schroeder
Representative, Colorado
sponsor, Citizens' Hearings for Radiation Victims

The existence of nuclear weapons is killing us. Their production contaminates our environment, destroys our natural resources, and depletes our human energy and creativity. But the most critical danger they represent is to life itself. Sickness, accidents, genetic damage and death, these are the real products of the nuclear arms race. We say no to the threat of global holocaust, no to the arms race, no to death. We say yes to a world where people, animals, plants and the earth itself are respected and valued.

Women's Encampment for a Future of Peace and Justice
Seneca Army Depot, New York
July 1983

C. Spiritual and Psychological Distress

Child abuse consists not only of violent acts toward children but also of threats of violence. The existence of nuclear weapons in our world represents global child abuse for those weapons threaten children with hideous personal injury and death.

As a result of this nuclear threat, mental health professionals are documenting disturbing children's behaviors of: terror, anger, despair, avoidance of involvement in personal relationships, and a gnawing fear they will never grow up. As adults, we have a responsibility to remove this threat.   **Patrick Gannon**

When we talk to today's children, they wonder if they have a future, and I think we have to wonder what we are doing. Our priorities are on the military and not on our nation's health.

Carol Nadelson
American Psychiatric Association

How are we supposed to start our lives with death looking over our shoulders?

Jessica
Age 17
In the Nuclear Shadow: What Can the Children Tell Us?

Sometimes it occurs to me that I might not grow up.

Anthony
Age 11
In the Nuclear Shadow: What Can the Children Tell Us?

Dear God,
   Adam was the first man on earth. I hope I'm not the last.

Billy K.
Chicago
Age 7
Please Save My World

I was on a camping trip in the fifth grade, and one kid started telling me that there were these bombs that could just wipe us all out. I felt sick. Ever since then I've been aware of things on TV, things people say, and it will pop up all of a sudden, on a nice day or when I'm having fun—I'll remember that it could all end in a minute.

Caedmon Fujimoto
Age 16
Our Future at Stake

The effects of nuclear weapons lie in our heads as well as in radioactive fallout. The damage that is being done *now* to people's vision of the future and their faith in future generations is incalculable.

Alice Cook and Gwyn Kirk
Greenham Women Everywhere

Young people are trying to find their way in a troubled and complex society. But hopeful signs are few, and the participants feel relatively powerless to influence events.

Stanley Elam
"Educators and the Nuclear Threat"
Phi Delta Kappan

When young people are deprived of an opportunity to give their lives a meaning, and when they have lost their last glimmer of hope, they fall victims to drugs and crime.

Declaration of the International
Meeting of Latin American Bishops
November/December 1977

* Men have brought their powers of subduing the forces of nature to such a pitch that by using them, they could now very easily exterminate one another to the last man. They know this—hence arises a great part of their current unrest, their dejection, their mood of apprehension.

Sigmund Freud
Civilization and Its Discontents

I am a child psychologist and author of books on how children's intelligence develops. Lately I have been doing some research on the effects of the nuclear threat on children's thinking, and it worries me greatly...

Mary Ann Pulaski

I worry too much about nuclear war and I'm too young to worry.

Billy C.
Las Vegas
Age 7
Please Save My World

I don't want to be the last person on earth because then I will have nobody to play with.

Laura R.
Buffalo
Age 6
Please Save My World

If everybody in the world says that they want peace how can we still have nuclear bombs? Somebody in the world must be lying.

Joan G.
Brooklyn
Age 10
Please Save My World

Since I learned about the bomb I don't smile so much any more.

Judith K.
Nashville
Age 7
Please Save My World

Depression is not sobbing and crying and giving vent. It is plain and simple reduction of feeling.

Judith Guest
Ordinary People

Given the social taboo against crying out [over the threat of nuclear annihilation] people distance themselves from each other as do the families and friends of the terminally ill.

Harvey Cox

You can't love someone if you don't think you will have them long.
teenage girl
In the Nuclear Shadow: What Can the Children Tell Us?

We are a society caught between a sense of impending apocalypse and an inability to acknowledge it. The refusal of feeling takes a heavy toll. The toll is not only an impoverishment of emotional and sensory life—the flowers dimmer and less fragrant, loves less ecstatic. This psychic numbing also impedes the capacity to process and respond to information. The energy expended in pushing down despair is diverted from more creative uses. We erect an invisible screen, selectively filtering out anxiety-provoking data. In a world where organisms require feedback in order to adapt and survive, this is suicidal.
Joanna Macy

...I am often too scared or depressed to want to meet this issue head on...
Kay Copenhauer

The schools I went to never talked about nuclear weapons or Hiroshima or the arms race. I think maybe teachers were afraid to talk about it. It made me think it just wasn't a big deal to them, or it wasn't important, or they were afraid. But that seemed strange to me....It's not like we don't hear about nuclear weapons. It's on the news, it's in the papers, it's on television. But people act like we aren't supposed to talk about it.
Ursell Austin
Age 16
Our Future at Stake

Other kids should know that if we don't do something soon, terrible things will happen. They should know about the dangers of nuclear weapons and also that there are things we can do to prevent a nuclear war....At first I was scared to bring it up, but now I do it. Sometimes I try to talk to people but they don't want to hear it. I think they are scared to face reality. That makes me really sad.
Regina Hunter
Age 15
Our Future at Stake

The Americans are forcing even their friends into becoming their enemies. It is curious that the Americans, who calculate so carefully on the possibilities of military victory, do not realize that in the process they are incurring deep psychological and political defeat. The image of America will never again be the image of revolution, freedom, and democracy, but the image of violence and militarism.
Martin Luther King, Jr.

The problem in defense is how far you can go without destroying from within what you are trying to defend from without.

Dwight D. Eisenhower

A nation that continues to spend more money on military defense than on programs of social uplift is approaching spiritual death.

Martin Luther King, Jr.

ADDITIONS:

8
The Lighter Side
of a Serious Subject

You ask if we need anything—Ann wants an elephant, Nancy and I would like a Xerox machine, and I'll take a piano. Also if you could spread some farm animals around the lawn so the rooster alarm clock can function I'll feel right at home....We want a bouquet of wildflowers, world peace, and 27 people to go over the ELF fence....If you are unable to fulfill all these wishes, we'll take a watermelon instead.

Kathy Kelly
letter from Ashland County jail
July 1985

I am for a nuclear freeze. Even in the summertime.

Andy K.
Seattle, Age 8
Please Save My World

Dear Mr. President,
   Please wear mittens in the White House so you won't be able to put your finger on the button.

Andy S.
San Francisco, Age 9
Please Save My World

Received at Disneyland—a letter from the Selective Service System addressed to Mickey M. Mouse and opening with these words: "Dear Registrant: Our records indicate you have not responded to our initial request for necessary date of birth information..."

The Progressive

Some white folks I just can't understand. They're more concerned about busing a kid to school than they are about shipping a kid to Vietnam....That's like worrying about dandruff when you've got cancer of the eyeballs.

Dick Gregory
Write Me In

Being a pacifist between wars is as easy as being a vegetarian between meals.

Ammon Hennacy

"Peace" is that period of cheating between battles.

Ambrose Bierce
The Devil's Dictionary

Two things I am afraid of—the bomb and the dentist.

Holly G.
Seattle, Age 7
Please Save My World

Advertisement before a nuclear attack:
RUN FOR YOUR LIFE!
You've always been careful when it comes to your health.
You've jogged.
You've done the marathon in under three.
You're a leader. A winner. A survivor. A runner.
So when your life depends on it you'll want running shoes that give you
blast-off capability equal to the situation.
NUKES
The *Nuke* running shoe has a unique deep-waffle sole that gives you that
extra spring you need to go from Ground Zero to Mile 20 in just five
seconds. Break in a pair of *Nukes* today. You might be there to be glad
you did.

Meet Mr. Bomb
A Practical Guide to Nuclear Extinction

Depending on your distance from ground zero, you could experience
temperatures of up to 4000 degrees Centigrade. Why not prepare for this
by spending 10 to 15 minutes a day in your clothes dryer?

Meet Mr. Bomb
A Practical Guide to Nuclear Extinction

Blast is actually no worse than if a 500,000-ton baseball, hit on a line
drive, were to strike your home.

Meet Mr. Bomb
A Practical Guide to Nuclear Extinction

An effective shelter should be strong enough to withstand a direct hit by
a five-megaton warhead....The new super material developed by NASA
for use in the space shuttle is the only building material that can meet
this requirement. Two-by-four panels of the metal can be purchased from
most aerospace manufacturers....A typical 2000 square foot residence
can be made bomb-proof with about 5000 panels at a cost of $3.4 million.
Most banks will be happy to give you a home improvement loan to
finance your new shielding...

Meet Mr. Bomb
A Practical Guide to Nuclear Extinction

For more information write INSANE, Washington D.C. INSANE
(Interested Non-seditious Americans for a Nuclear Event) is a prominent
anti-freeze group.

Meet Mr. Bomb
A Practical Guide to Nuclear Extinction

I am not very keen for doves or hawks. I think we need more owls.

George Aiken

Dear God:
Please save the world. Even if you're not crazy about it.
                                                    Lionel T.
                                                    Hershey, Age 8
                                                    Please Save My World

How I Would Save the World
First, I would take all the generals and put them in a big boat in the middle of the ocean. Then I would forget to pick them up.
                                                    Robert Stuart
                                                    Age 9
                                                    Please Save My World

---

Reporter: Mr. Gandhi, what do you think of Western Civilization?
Mr. Gandhi: I think it would be a good idea!

---

* More than any other time in history, mankind faces the crossroads...one path leads to despair and utter hopelessness, the other to total extinction. I pray we have the wisdom to choose wisely.
                                                    Woody Allen

Pray for the dead, and fight like hell for the living.
                                                    Mary Harris "Mother " Jones

The thing about peace work is the hours are long...but the pay is really lousy.
                                                    Barb Katt

We pray for peace every Sunday at Church. Everybody at Church prays for peace. Even the people who are sleeping.
                                                    Eric W.
                                                    New York, Age 9
                                                    Please Save My World

My hometown is the hotbed of social rest.
                                                    Anonymous

Well, you lose some...and you lose some.
                                                    Sister Marjorie Tuite

We should lock up all the bombs in a bank then nobody could get them because nobody can get into a bank.
                                                    Annie G.
                                                    Baldwin, Age 7
                                                    Please Save My World

The trouble with good ideas is that they quickly degenerate into hard work.

Anonymous

Little children and animals don't want war. Only grownups and crocodiles.

Anthony R.
Atlanta, Age 10
Please Save My World

SMILE! We're one day closer to World Disarmament—and a real big party.

Anonymous

ADDITIONS:

ADDITIONS:

9
National Ideals

The people we call our "founders" are often referred to as "rebels," "radicals," "patriots," or "revolutionaries."

Voices of the American Revolution

* We hold these truths to be self-evident, that all men are created equal; that they are endowed by their Creator with certain unalienable rights; that among these are life, liberty, and the pursuit of happiness. That, to secure these rights, governments are instituted among men, deriving their just powers from the consent of the governed; that, whenever any form of government becomes destructive of these ends, it is the right of the people to alter or to abolish it, and to institute a new government, laying its foundation on such principles, and organizing its powers in such form, as to them shall seem most likely to effect their safety and happiness...experience hath shown, that mankind are more disposed to suffer...than to right themselves by abolishing the forms to which they are accustomed...it is their right, it is their duty, to throw off such government, and to provide new guards for their future security.

**Declaration of Independence
July 1776**

The care of life and happiness, and not their destruction, is the first and only legitimate object of good government.

Thomas Jefferson

Some boast of being friends to government; I am a friend to righteous government founded upon the principles of reason and justice; but I glory in publicly avowing my eternal enmity to tyranny.

**John Hancock
1774**

...may [our] country itself become a vast and splendid monument, not of oppression and terror, but of wisdom, of peace, and of liberty...

Daniel Webster

Those who are desirous of enjoying all the advantages of liberty themselves, should be willing to extend personal liberties to others.

**Rhode Island Assembly
1774**

* I have always strenuously supported the right of every man to his opinion, however different that opinion might be to mine. He who denies to another this right, makes a slave of himself to his present opinion, because he precludes himself the right of changing it.

Thomas Paine

The government of the United States of America is not in any sense founded on the Christian religion.

George Washington

When shall it be said in any country of the world, my poor are happy; neither ignorance or distress is to be found among them; my jails are empty of prisoners, my streets of beggars; the aged are not in want, the taxes are not oppressive; the rational world is my friend, because I am the friend of its happiness; when these things can be said, then may that country boast of its constitution and government.

Thomas Paine

True patriotism hates injustice in its own land more than anywhere else.

Clarence Darrow

* What has commonly been called rebellion has more often been nothing but a glorious struggle in opposition to the lawless power of rebellious kings and princes.

Sam Adams, 1776

The American war is over; but this is far from the case with the American Revolution. On the contrary, nothing but the first act of the great drama is closed.

Benjamin Rush, 1787

God forbid we should ever be twenty years without a rebellion.

Thomas Jefferson, 1787

A sanguine confidence in the future has been a hallmark of the American character and a source of national pride.

Joanna Rogers Macy

ADDITIONS:

ADDITIONS:

10
Forsaken Ideals

To sleep, perchance to dream, aye, there's the rub.
To fight, perchance to win, aye, there's the rub.
For victory brings power and prestige
And the children of the children of the fighters take all for granted and
in turn oppress.

Pete Seeger

There is no other measure by which to validate government save for its
contribution to life. The government that fails by this standard has
violated its troth. It is illegitimate. It is a threat to the people.

Terry Herndon
Teacher

Rulers have no authority from God to do mischief.

Jonathan Mayhew, 1750

* Civil tyranny is usually small in its beginning, like the "drop in the
bucket," till at length, like a mighty torrent of raging waves of the sea,
it bears down all before it and deluges whole countries and
empires....Tyranny brings ignorance and brutality along with it. It
degrades men from their just rank into the class of brutes. It dampens
their spirits. It suppresses arts. It extinguishes every spark of noble ardor
and generosity in the breasts of those who are enslaved by it. It makes
naturally strong and great minds feeble and little and triumphs over the
ruins of virtue and humanity. This is true of tyranny in every shape.
There can be nothing great and good where its influence reaches.

Jonathan Mayhew, 1750

I believe there are more instances of the abridgement of the freedom of
the people by gradual and silent encroachments of those in power than
by violent and sudden usurpations.

James Madison

When an act injurious to freedom has once been done, and the people
bear it, the repetition of it is most likely to meet with submission. For
as the mischief of the one was found to be tolerable, they will hope that
of the second will prove so too; and they will not regard the infamy of
the last, because they are stained with that of the first.

John Dickinson, 1768

* If the liberties of America are ever completely ruined it will in all
probability be the consequence of a mistaken notion of prudence, which
leads men to acquiesce in measures of the most destructive tendency for
the sake of present ease. When designs are formed to raze the very
foundation of a free government, those few who are to erect their grandeur
and fortunes upon the general ruin will employ every art to soothe the
devoted people into a state of indolence, inattention and security, which
is forever the forerunner of slavery....And it has been an old game played

over and over again to hold up the men who would rouse their fellow citizens and countrymen...as "pretended patriots," "intemperate politicians," "rash, hot-headed men," "wretched desperados."

Sam Adams, 1771

If once the people become inattentive to the public affairs, you and I and Congress and assemblies, judges and governors, shall all become wolves.

Thomas Jefferson, 1787

* All pretenders to government which have not ultimately the good of the governed in view and do not afford, or endeavor to afford, protection to those over whom they pretend such claims, should, instead of the respects due to legislatures, courts and the like, be esteemed and treated as enemies to society and the rights of mankind.

Ethan Allen, 1780

Tyranny and oppression are just as possible under democratic forms as under any other. We are slow to realize that democracy is a life and involves continual struggle.

Robert M. La Follette

...if totalitarianism comes to this country, it will surely do so in the guise of 100% Americanism.

Huey Long

When fascism comes to the United States, it'll be because the people voted it in.

Irving Wallace
The R Amendment

We despise totalitarianism so much that we are willing to become totalitarian to destroy it.

American Friends Service Committee
Speak Truth to Power

The House Un-American Activities Committee is the most un-American thing in America.

Harry S. Truman

* As soon as men decide that all means are permitted to fight an evil, then their good becomes indistinguishable from the evil that they set out to destroy.

Christopher Dawson
The Judgement of Nations

ADDITIONS:

11
Military Might

The great oppressors of the earth were entrusted with power by the people to defend them from the little oppressors. The sword of justice was put into their hands, but behold they soon turned it into a sword of oppression.

Samuel Webster, 1777

Though it has been said that a standing army is necessary for the dignity and safety of America, freedom revolts at the idea. Standing armies have been the nursery of vice and the bane of liberty from the Roman Legions to the planting of British cohorts in the capitals of America.

Mercy Warren, 1788

The spirit of this country is totally adverse to a large military force.

Thomas Jefferson, 1807

Tyrants always support themselves with standing armies!

Samuel Webster, 1777

Nothing can be more aggravated than for the shepherds to mislead and butcher the flock they were set to defend and feed.

Samuel Webster, 1777

If there be one principle more deeply rooted than any other in the mind of every American, it is that we should have nothing to do with conquest.

Thomas Jefferson

Observe good faith and justice towards all nations; cultivate peace and harmony with all.

George Washington
Farewell Address
1796

ADDITIONS:

12
Freedom of the Press

In establishing American independence, the pen and the press had merit equal to that of the sword.

David Ramsay, 1783

The liberty of the press is essential to the security of freedom in a state. It ought not, therefore, be restrained.

Massachusetts Bill of Rights, 1780

...no government ought to be without critics and where the press is free no one ever will.

Thomas Jefferson, 1791

The only security of all is a free press. The force of public opinion cannot be resisted, when permitted freely to be expressed. The agitation it produces must be submitted to. It is necessary to keep the waters pure.

Thomas Jefferson, 1823

Should the liberty of the press be once destroyed, farewell to the remainder of our invaluable rights and privileges.

Isaiah Thomas, 1700s

ADDITIONS:

13
Informed Citizens

Enlighten the people generally, and tyranny and oppressions of body and mind will vanish like evil spirits at the dawn of day.

Thomas Jefferson, 1816

* ...it is the practice of the new world, America, to make men as wise as possible, so that their knowledge being complete, they may be rationally governed.

Tom Paine, 1778

Liberty cannot be preserved without a general knowledge among the people.

John Adams, 1767

It is a shame, a scandal to civilized society, that part only of the citizens should be sent to colleges and universities, to learn to cheat the rest of their liberties.

Robert Coram, 1791

Neither piety, virtue, or liberty can long flourish in a community where the education of youth is neglected.

Samuel Cooper, 1780

If science produces no better fruits than tyranny, murder, rapine and destitution of national morality, I would rather wish our country to remain ignorant.

Thomas Jefferson

Where learning is confined to a few people, we always find monarchy, aristocracy and slavery.

Benjamin Rush, 1786

ADDITIONS:

14
Big Business

I hope we shall crush in its birth the aristocracy of our moneyed corporations, which dare already to challenge our government to a trial of strength and bid defiance to the laws of our country.

Thomas Jefferson, 1814

* Experience declares that man is the only animal which devours his own kind, for I can apply no milder term...to the general prey of the rich on the poor.

Thomas Jefferson, 1787

[Monopolies are] odious, contrary to the principles of a free government, and the principles of commerce.

Maryland Revolutionary Constitution, 1776

* Government is instituted for the protection, safety, and happiness of the people, and not for the profit, honour, or private interest of any man, family, or class of men.

Mercy Warren, 1788

Harmony, and a liberal intercourse with all nations, are recommended by policy, humanity, and interest. But even our commercial policy should hold an equal and impartial hand; neither seeking or granting exclusive favors or preferences; consulting the natural course of things; diffusing and diversifying, by gentle means, the streams of commerce, but forcing nothing...

George Washington
Farewell Address, 1796

* The protection of a man's person is more sacred than the protection of property.

Tom Paine
***The Rights of Man*, 1792**

ADDITIONS:

15
False Patriotism

Guard against the postures of pretended patriotism.

**George Washington
1796**

I venture to suggest that patriotism is not a short and frenzied outburst of emotion, but the tranquil and steady dedication of a lifetime.

Adlai E. Stevenson

* Let the history of the Federal Government instruct mankind that the mask of patriotism may be worn to conceal the foulest designs against the liberties of the people.

**Benjamin Bache
1798**

Patriotism is the finest flower of western civilization as well as the refuge of the scoundrel.

Leonard Woolf

* Patriotism is not, as sentimentalists like to assert, one of the profoundest of man's noblest instincts.

Ida Alexa Ross Wylie

Patriotism is the last refuge of a scoundrel.

Samuel Johnson

Christian faith makes uncritical patriotism impossible.

Peter Monkres

A people living under the perpetual menace of war and invasion is very easy to govern. It demands no social reforms. It does not haggle over expenditures on armaments and military equipment. It pays without discussion, it ruins itself, and that is an excellent thing for the syndicates of financiers and manufacturers for whom patriotic terrors are an abundant source of gain.

Anatole France

* I am persuaded that there is absolutely no limit in the absurdities that can, by government action, come to be generally believed. Give me an adequate army, with power to provide it with more pay and better food than falls to the lot of the average man, and I will undertake, within thirty years, to make the majority of the population believe that two and two are three, that water freezes when it gets hot and boils when it gets cold, or any other nonsense that might seem to serve the interest of the State. Of course, even when these beliefs had been generated, people would not put the kettle in the refrigerator when they wanted it to boil. That cold makes water boil would be a Sunday truth, sacred and mystical, to be professed in awed tones, but not to be acted on in daily life. What would happen would be that any verbal denial of the mystic doctrine

would be made illegal, and obstinate heretics would be "frozen" at the stake. No person who did not enthusiastically accept the official doctrine would be allowed to teach or to have any position of power. Only the very highest officials, in their cups, would whisper to each other what rubbish it all is; then they would laugh and drink again.

Bertrand Russell
Unpopular Essays
1950

* Why of course the people don't want war. Why should some poor slob on a farm want to risk his life in a war when the best he can get out of it is to come back to his farm in one piece? Naturally the common people don't want war: Neither in Russia, nor in England, nor for that matter in Germany. That is understood. But after all, it is the leaders of the country who determine the policy and it is always a simple matter to drag the people along, whether it is a democracy, or a fascist dictatorship, or a parliament, or a communist dictatorship. Voice or no voice, the people can always be brought to the bidding of the leaders. That is easy. All you have to do is tell them they are being attacked, and denounce the pacifists for lack of patriotism and exposing the country to danger. It works the same in any country.

Hermann Goering
Hitler's Deputy

ADDITIONS:

ADDITIONS:

16
Love It and Change It

Our country, right or wrong. When right, to be kept right; when wrong, to be put right.

Carl Schurz
famous German immigrant

* Truth is great and will prevail if left to herself...she is the proper and sufficient antagonist to error, and has nothing to fear from the conflict unless by human interposition disarmed of her natural weapons, free argument and debate.

Thomas Jefferson

The origin of all power is in the people, and...they have an incontestible right to check the creatures of their own creation.

Mercy Warren
1788

Sir, I would rather be right than be President.

Henry Clay

The real patriots are those who love America as she is, but who want the beloved to be more lovable. This is not treachery. This, as every parent, every teacher, every friend must know, is the truest and noblest affection.

Adlai E. Stevenson

It is un-American *not* to criticize your country when it does wrong.

Clergy and Laity Concerned

Criticism is more than a right; it is an act of patriotism—a higher form of patriotism, I believe, than the familiar ritual of national adulation. All of us have the responsibility to act upon the higher patriotism which is to love our country less for what it is than for what we would like it to be.

William Fulbright
former Senator, Arkansas

* The real patriot is the person who is not afraid to criticize the defective policies of the country which he loves.

Joseph J. Fahey

* It is the duty of every good citizen to point out what he thinks erroneous in the commonwealth.

James Otis
1764

I can't see how not wanting to blow up the world is un-American.

William Winpisinger
President
International Association of Machinists and Aerospace Workers

If it is un-American to be against arms build-ups that are created primarily to give more power to the military and more hefty profits to arms manufacturers, then yes, we are un-American.

Clergy and Laity Concerned

I should like to be able to love my country and still love justice.

Albert Camus

The love of one's country is a splendid thing. But why should love stop at the border?

Pablo Casals

If we are to be leaders—Number 1—let it be as an example of a government concerned with the dignity and growth of people everywhere.

Madge Micheels-Cyrus

America is great because America is good and if America ever ceases to be good, America will cease to be great.

Alexis de Tocqueville

America must choose one of three courses after this war: narrow nationalism, which inevitably means the ultimate loss of our own liberty; international imperialism, which means the sacrifice of some other nation's liberty; or the creation of a world in which there shall be an equality of opportunity for every race and every nation.

Wendell L. Wilkie, 1940s

Nothing less than a global patriotism is demanded in the 3rd century of the U.S.....*all* people are created equal. Any "more perfect union" must involve the whole human family. Our quest for "domestic tranquility" must recognize the globe as our common domicile.

Philip Scharper
The Patriot's Bible

ADDITIONS:

ADDITIONS:

17
Bumperstickers,
Buttons,
T-Shirts,
and Graffiti

Nuclear weapons
May They Rust in Peace

                                          Bread Not Bombs

If the people lead,
eventually the leaders will follow.

                                          Stop the Arms Race
                                          Not the Human Race

Military Intelligence
is a contradiction in terms.

                                          Think Globally
                                          Act Locally

Uranium
Leave It In The Ground

                                          Plutonium
                                          is Forever

We don't want nuclear waste here;
So don't make it anywhere.

                                          Better Active Today
                                          Than Radioactive Tomorrow

Split Wood
Not Atoms

                                          Solar Employs
                                          Nuclear Destroys

No Nukes is
Good Nukes

                                          Wearing Buttons
                                          Is Not Enough

War is not healthy for children and other living things.
Another Mother for Peace

                                          Child Care
                                          Not Warfare

You can't hug your kids with nuclear arms.

Arms Are For Linking

Arms Are For Embracing

I Want To Grow Up
Not Blow Up

Give Children Dreams
Not Nuclear Nightmares

Bombs Scare Bears

This House Has No Fallout Shelter
Peace Is Our Only Security

There Is No Silver Lining
In A Mushroom Cloud

Nuclear war is bad for peace of mind
Nuclear war is bad for war veterans
Nuclear war is bad for international relations
Nuclear war is bad for real estate
Nuclear war is good for nothing
The Hundredth Monkey

In Every War
There's A Hiroshima
Waiting To Happen

Hands off Outer Space
Star Wars "Defense"
An Offensive, Deadly Lie

Peace on earth
and in space

Military Solutions Are Problems

El Salvador is Spanish for Vietnam.

Join the Army;
travel to exotic, distant lands;
meet exciting, unusual people—and kill them.

Don't Register
For World War III
The War Without Winners

Support Your Local
Draft Resister

They can jail the resister,
but not the resistance.

Why do we kill people who kill people
to prove that killing people is wrong?

America: Love it or leave it.

America: Love it and change it.

Peace is Patriotic

Peace is growing

Civil Disobedience
is Civil Defense

Peace In The World
Or The World In Pieces

Be All You Can Be
Work For Peace

The Moral Majority Is Neither

No One Is Right
If No One Is Left

WAR doesn't decide who's right
—only who's left.

Minds are like parachutes; they only function when they are open.

Kites rise highest
against the wind.

Help Cure America's
Military-Industrial Complex

The government says 140,000,000 deaths are acceptable in a nuclear war. The question is, is the government acceptable?
Minnesota Nuclear Freeze Campaign

Nuclear war can spoil
your whole day.

* God made heaven and earth in six days.
Man can destroy it in six minutes.

I haven't learned to live with the bomb.

War Is Costly
Peace Is Priceless

Teach peace.

Legalize peace.

Feed The Cities
Not The Pentagon

Save the Nukes
No Whales

Extinct is Forever

Live Simply
That Others May
Simply Live

Violence Ends
Where Love Begins

The Meek
Are Getting Ready

"Meek" Ain't Weak

Be Realistic
Demand The Impossible

Peace is Possible.

Create Peace

World War III
Cancelled by Popular Demand

Vision Or Fission

Save The World?
...You Bet!

Without World Disarmament...Who Will Have Grandchildren?
Women's International League For Peace And Freedom

Hope springs maternal.
Another Mother for Peace

ADDITIONS:

18
Earth As One

* No man is an island, entire of itself....any man's death diminishes me, because I am involved in mankind; and therefore never send to know for whom the bell tolls; it tolls for thee.

John Donne

I am one with this planet.
I am one with all people.
I am one with all life.

Rusty Schweickart
Apollo Astronaut

* There is a destiny that makes us brothers;
    None goes his way alone;
  All that we send into the lives of others
    Comes back into our own.

Edwin Markham

* We were born to unite with our fellow men, and to join in community with the human race.

Cicero
Definibus, **IV**

* Don't become your brother's keeper, be your brother's brother.

Jesse Jackson

Something broke for me Wednesday, a thunderstorm of the heart, when we were at the gate early, keening. Fingering the barbed wire along the top of the fence, I felt all the fences that separate us humans, all the barbs of ignorance and violence...culminating in our casual consideration of blowing up our planet-home. There was a great healing then in my sobbing on that poisoned land, at seeing the tears of the women around me spill down with my own.

Andi Scott
Women's Peace Encampment, Seneca Falls, NY
1983

It is "isolation" that is critical to war. You can't be abusive when you realize your connectedness.

David Kadlec

Peace is inclusive.

Madge Micheels-Cyrus

No peace which is not peace for all, no rest till all has been fulfilled.

Dag Hammarskjöld

We are all members of one family, yesterday, today, and tomorrow. We know we shall find peace only where we find justice—only where we find respect for all human beings, only where all human beings have the right to a decent living for themselves and their families.

The "Snarlers" of the Perús Cement Company
Brazil, 1974
Christ in a Poncho

We have learned that we cannot live alone, at peace; that our own well-being is dependent upon the well-being of other nations, far away.

Franklin Delano Roosevelt

Especially important it is to realize that there can be no assured peace and tranquility for any one nation except as it is achieved for all. So long as want, frustration and a sense of injustice prevail among significant sections of the earth, no other section can be wholly released from fear.

Dwight D. Eisenhower

The social progress, order, security and peace of each country are necessarily connected with the social progress, order, security and peace of all other countries.

Pope John XXIII

Injustice anywhere is a threat to justice everywhere. We are caught in an inescapable network of mutuality, tied in a single garment of destiny.

Martin Luther King, Jr.
Letter from a Birmingham Jail

* You can only protect your liberties in this world by protecting the other man's freedom. You can only be free if I am free.

Clarence Darrow

...while there is a lower class, I am in it; while there is a criminal element, I am of it; while there is a soul in prison, I am not free.

Eugene Debs

The good we secure for ourselves is precarious and uncertain...until it is secured for all of us and incorporated into our common life.

Jane Addams
Nobel Peace Prize, 1931

Where nature makes natural allies of us all, we can demonstrate that beneficial relations are possible even with those with whom we most deeply disagree, and this must someday be the basis of world peace and world law.

John F. Kennedy

If we cannot end our differences, at least we can help make the world safe for diversity. For, in the final analysis, our most basic common link is that we all inhabit this small planet. We all breathe the same air. We all cherish our children's future. And we are all mortal.

John F. Kennedy

* The wave of the future is not the conquest of the world by a single dogmatic creed but the liberation of the diverse energies of free nations and free men.

John F. Kennedy

* All your strength is in your union.
All your danger is in discord.
Therefore be at peace henceforward.
And as brothers live together.

Henry Wadsworth Longfellow
The Song of Hiawatha

* One of the most moving letters in the New Testament was the Apostle Paul's letter to the churches at Galatia, in which he wrote:
There is neither Jew nor Greek.
There is neither slave nor free.
There is neither male nor female.
You are all one.
And we add there is neither Russian nor American, for all are one. "All are Abraham's offspring. All are heirs, according to the promise."

Philip Zwerling

There are no Communist babies. There are no Capitalist babies.

Jackie Rivet-River

No ideological or political doctrine should be considered more important than life and love of our fellow human beings. Without ideological and political doctrines we can still live in peace, but without respect for life, the world will be destroyed.

Thich Thien Minh

The basic problem is not political, it is apolitical and human. One of the most important things to do is to keep cutting deliberately through political lines and barriers and emphasizing that these are largely fabrications and that there is a genuine reality: the human dimension.

Thomas Merton

From her father, Jane learned that "the things that make us alike are stronger than the things that make us different." **Dorothy Nathan**
Women of Courage
written about Jane Addams

It is we human beings who have made pigmentation a leprosy in our lives instead of a gift. **Anonymous**

Our lives extend beyond our skins, in radical interdependence with the rest of the world.

Joanna Rogers Macy

Though I am different from you, we were born involved in one another.

T'ao Chien

We cannot live for ourselves alone. Our lives are connected by a thousand invisible threads, and along these sympathetic fibers, our actions run as causes and return to us as results...

Herman Melville

When we try to pick out something by itself, we find it hitched to everything else in the Universe.

John Muir

We are one, after all, you and I; together we suffer, together exist, and forever will recreate each other.

Teilhard de Chardin

I would like us to be interventionists everywhere in the world. I would like to intervene everywhere with whatever benefits we've had from living in this land—health care, education, housing. We also need to learn from those people, learn how their cultures have prospered in the past, learn from their mistakes and their successes. We ought to be actively involved everywhere in the world all the time, but not militarily.

Rear Admiral Gene R. La Rocque
U.S. Navy (retired)

* In every man there is something wherein I may learn of him, and in that I am his pupil.

Ralph Waldo Emerson

Let us unite, let us hold each other tightly, let us merge our hearts, let us create for Earth a brain and a heart, let us give a human meaning to the superhuman struggle.

Nikos Kazantzakis

The moment we cease to hold each other,
The moment we break faith with one another,
The sea engulfs us and the light goes out.

Anonymous

We have a long, long way to go. So let us hasten along the road, the roads of human tenderness and generosity. Groping, we may find one another's hands in the dark.

Emily Greene Balch

We're all part of the Great Holy mystery—all of us—and so we can't hate each other or we are hating ourselves.

Anonymous

The supreme reality of our time is our indivisibility as children of God and the common vulnerability of our planet.

John F. Kennedy

We travel together, passengers on a little spaceship, dependent on its vulnerable reserves of air and soil; all committed for our safety to its security and peace; preserved from annihilation only by the care, the work, and the love we give our fragile craft, and, I may say, each other.

Adlai E. Stevenson
his last speech

Nuclear holocaust is five minutes away. But maybe those minutes are the graced moment in which God is speaking to all of humanity. We have no option but to go the way of peace. Maybe God is using this threat to give us the opportunity to recognize our common humanity, to bring us into the one world, the one community, the one family of God.

Bishop Walter Sullivan
Sojourners
January 1982

Therefore if you insist upon fighting to protect me, or "our" country, let it be understood, soberly and rationally between us, that you are fighting to gratify a sex instinct which I cannot share; to procure benefits which I have not shared and probably will not share; but not to gratify my instincts, or to protect either myself or my country. For...in fact, as a woman, I have no country. As a woman, I want no country. As a woman, my country is the whole world.

Virginia Woolf
Three Guineas

People who develop the habit of thinking of themselves as world citizens are fulfilling the first requirement of sanity in our time.

Norman Cousins

* Our country is the world, our countrymen are all mankind.

William Lloyd Garrison

I'm not into isms and asms. There isn't a Catholic moon and a Baptist sun. I know the universal God is universal....I feel that the same God-force that is the mother and father of the Pope is also the mother and father of the loneliest wino on the planet.

Dick Gregory

We appeal, as human beings to human beings: Remember your humanity, and forget the rest.

in a statement signed by
Bertrand Russell, Albert Einstein, and others

ADDITIONS:

ADDITIONS:

19
Earth Keeping

...peace, not conflict, is the prevailing mode of life in nature: 95 percent of all living beings die naturally of old age or sickness (without human interference), and violence causes only 5 percent of all deaths.

Sydney J. Harris

Peace on and with the earth. For all its children.

The Second Biennial Conference on the Fate of the Earth

* The earth-mother had many children other than men: the stem of long wild grass that developed into a stalk of maize, the lofty spruce, all the birds of the air, the beasts of the plain and forest, the insect and the ant. They too had equal rights to life.

Hopi Legend
Frank Waters
The American Indian Speaks

A weed is nothing more than a flower in disguise.

Jane Russell Lowell

Treat the earth well...it was not given to you by your parents....It was lent to you by your children.

Kenyan Proverb

In our every deliberation, we must consider the impact of our decisions on the next seven generations...on those faces that are yet beneath the ground.

The Great Law of the Six Nations Iroquois Confederacy

* We seek a renewed stirring of love for the earth. We urge that what man is capable of doing to the earth is not always what he ought to do, and we plead that all people, here, now determine that a wide, spacious untrammeled freedom shall remain as living testimony that this generation, *our own*, had *love* for the next.

David Brower

...we need to preserve a few places, a few samples of primeval country so that when the pace gets too fast we can look at it, think about it, contemplate it, and somehow restore equanimity to our souls.

Sigurd Olson

So many major structures of belief have arisen at least in part from experiences in wilderness....Moses, Jesus and Mohammed in the desert mountains, Siddhartha in the jungle...the five year wilderness voyage of a Victorian amateur naturalist named Charles Darwin. There evidently is more to wilderness than meets the eye...psychic raw materials from which every age has cut, dammed or quarried an invisible civilization....

David Rains Wallace
The Klamath Knot

We face the question whether a still higher "standard of living" is worth its cost in things natural, wild and free. For us of the minority, the opportunity to see geese is more important than television, and the chance to find a pasque-flower is a right as inalienable as free speech.

Aldo Leopold

We sang songs that carried in their melodies all the sounds of nature—the running of waters, the sighing of winds, and the calls of the animals. Teach these to your children that they may come to love nature as we love it.

Grand Council Fire of American Indians
to the Mayor of Chicago
December 1927

To us peple the woods and the big hills and the Northern lights and the sunsets are all alive and we live with these things and live in the spirit of the woods like no white person can do. The big lakes we travel on, the little lonely lakes we set our beaver traps on with a ring of big black pines standin in rows lookin always north, like they were watchin for somethin that never comes, same as the Injun, they are real to us and when we are alone we speak to them and are not lonesome, only thinkin always of the long ago days and the old men. So we live in the past and the rest of the world keeps goin by. For all their modern inventions they cant live the way we do and they die if they try because they cant read the sunset and hear the old men talk in the wind.

Anaquoness
Ojibway, wounded while serving in France in WWI
February 1918

* The smallest mosquito is more wonderful than anything man will ever produce. So man must never lose his sense of the marvelousness of the world around and inside him—a world which he has not made and which, assuredly, has not made itself. Such an attitude engenders a spirit of nonviolence...

E. F. Schumacher

I never kill a bird or other animal without feeling bad inside. All true hunters must have that feeling that prevents them from killing just for killing's sake. There is no fun in just destroying life, and the Great Spirit puts that shadow in your heart when you destroy his creatures.

Joe Friday
Woods Cree Indian

With riches has come inexcusable waste. We have squandered a great part of what we might have used and have not stopped to conserve the exceeding bounty of nature, without which our genius for enterprise would have been worthless and impotent.

Woodrow Wilson

Garbage is not something you throw away. There is no such place as away. Disposal is a myth...

Nancy Cosper
Knowing Home

Every now and then I am impressed with the thinking of the non-Indian. I was in Cleveland...talking with a non-Indian about American history. He said that he was really sorry about what had happened to Indians, but that there was good reason for it. The continent had to be developed and he felt that Indians had stood in the way and thus had to be removed. "After all," he remarked, "what did you do with the land when you had it?" I didn't understand him until later when I discovered that the Cayahoga River running through Cleveland is inflammable. So many combustible pollutants are dumped into the river that the inhabitants have to take special precautions during the summer to avoid accidentally setting it on fire. After reviewing the argument of my non-Indian friend I decided that he was probably correct. Whites had made better use of the land. How many Indians could have thought of creating an inflammable river?

Vine Deloria, Jr.
We Talk, You Listen

Our honeymoon with the planet earth is over. We must take our marriage with the earth seriously. We cannot divorce it, but it can divorce us!

Grandon Harris

* How can the spirit of the earth like the white man?...Everywhere the white man has touched it, it is sore.

Wintu woman
Touch the Earth

We have probed the earth, excavated it, burned it, ripped things from it, buried things in it, chopped down its forests, leveled its hills, muddied its waters and dirtied its air. That does not fit my definition of a good tenant. If we were here on a month to month basis, we would have been evicted long ago.

Rose Bird
Chief Justice
California Supreme Court

An environmental setting developed over millions of years must be considered to have some merit. Anything so complicated as a planet, inhabited by more than a million and a half species of plants and animals, all of them living together in a more or less balanced equilibrium in which they continually use and reuse the same molecules of the soil and air, cannot be improved by aimless and uninformed tinkering.

E. F. Schumacher
Small Is Beautiful

* [According to the Bible] man was created in God's own image and divinely commanded to subdue the earth....We have so denuded the grasslands and forested mountains that the topsoil is washing down the drain into the sea. The underground water level is lowering so rapidly that we are being forced to develop means for purifying sea water for our use. The very air we breathe is becoming dangerously toxic in all our cities, and radioactive fallout from our latest technological triumph is laying wide swaths around the whole planet.

Yet it is not enough to have subdued a continent and exhausted its natural resources. There still remains a vast domain of untouched nature in the universe—the other planets in outer space.

Frank Waters
The American Indian Speaks

When you have pollution in one place, it spreads all over. It spreads just as arthritis or cancer spreads in the body. The earth is sick now because the earth is being mistreated, and some of the problems that may occur, some of the natural disasters that might happen in the near future, are only the natural adjustments that have to take place to throw off the sickness.

Rolling Thunder
modern medicine man

* Man did not make the earth, and though he had a natural right to occupy it, he had no right to locate as his property in perpetuity, any part of it.

Tom Paine
1796

* The earth was created by the assistance of the sun, and it should be left as it was...the country was made without lines of demarcation and it is no man's business to divide it....I never said the land was mine to do with it as I chose. The one who has the right to dispose of it is the one who created it. I claim a right to live on my land, and accord you the privilege to live on yours.

Chief Joseph
Nez Percé

* Some of our chiefs make the claim that the land belongs to us. It is not what the Great Spirit told me. He told me that the lands belong to Him, that no people owns the land; that I was not to forget to tell this to the white people when I met them in council.

Kannekuk
Kickapoo prophet
1827
I Have Spoken

How can you buy or sell the sky, the warmth of the land? If we do not own the freshness of the air and the sparkle of the water, how can you buy them?

Chief Seattle
1854

The land was not tangible property to be owned, divided, and alienated at will. It was their Mother Earth from which they were born, on whose breast they were suckled, and to whose womb they were returned in a prenatal posture at death.

Hopi Legend
Frank Waters
The American Indian Speaks

The earth is part of my body, and I never gave up the earth.

Toohulhulsote
a Nez Percé prophet

Too many people don't know that when they harm the earth they harm themselves, nor do they realize that when they harm themselves, they harm the earth.

Rolling Thunder
a modern medicine man

* This we know. The earth does not belong to man; man belongs to the earth. This we know. All things are connected. Whatever befalls the earth befalls the sons of the earth. Man did not weave the web of life. He is merely a strand in it. Whatever he does to the web, he does to himself.

Chief Seattle
1854

* Man was not created apart from nature...but out of nature whose unconscious forces and instinctual drives still swayed him. So we, the white, while subduing nature, also tried to subdue the aspect of nature within ourself....Our own minds and bodies became the battleground of man against nature, man against God, and man against himself, divided into two warring selves: reason and instinct, the conscious and the unconscious....They had cut themselves off from the roots of life.

Frank Waters
The American Indian Speaks

* A man's heart away from nature becomes hard...lack of respect for growing, living things soon leads to lack of respect for humans too.

Lakota Belief
Touch the Earth

When we see land as a community to which we belong, we may begin to use it with love and respect.

Aldo Leopold

...understanding begins with love and respect. It begins with respect for the Great Spirit, and the Great Spirit is the life that is in all things—all the creatures and the plants and even the rocks and the mineral....Such respect is not a feeling or an attitude only. It's a way of life. Such respect means that we never stop realizing and never neglect to carry out our obligation to ourselves and our environment.

Rolling Thunder
a modern medicine man

* Man must recognize the necessity of co-operating with nature. He must temper his demands and use and conserve the natural living resources of this earth in a manner that alone can provide for the continuation of his civilization.

Fairfield Osborn

When we deal gently with the earth—even when we have thoughtlessly damaged it—we can repair our friendship with it.

René Dubos

* Nature is sovereign and man's inner nature is sovereign. Nature is to be respected. All life and every single living being is to be respected. That's the only answer.

Rolling Thunder
a modern medicine man

The nuclear peril is usually seen in isolation from the threats to other forms of life and their ecosystems, but in fact should be seen as the very center of the ecological crisis....Both the effort to preserve the environment and the effort to save the species from extinction by nuclear arms would be strengthened by this recognition. The nuclear question, which now stands in eerie seclusion from the rest of life, would gain a context, and the ecological movement...would gain the humanistic intent that should stand at the heart of its concern.

Jonathan Schell
The Fate of the Earth

* If, in a nuclear holocaust, anyone hid himself deep enough under the earth and stayed there long enough to survive, he would emerge into a dying natural environment. The vulnerability of the environment is the last word in the argument against the usefulness of shelters: there is no hole big enough to hide all of nature in.

Jonathan Schell

If animals could vote they would be against nuclear war.

Mark M.
Los Angeles, Age 7
Please Save My World

If we don't stop the bomb who will take care of the flowers?

Neil J.
Seattle, Age 9
Please Save My World

We are the curators of life on earth. We hold it in the palm of our hands.
And it is our ultimate responsibility as spiritual, and moral, feeling human
beings, and not as scientists, to save this planet.

Dr. Helen Caldicott

If we do not speak for Earth, who will? If we are not committed to our
own survival, who will be?

Carl Sagan
Cosmos

* The frog does not drink up the pond in which he lives.

Native American proverb

Any scientist can testify that a dead ocean means a dead planet....No
national law, no national precautions can save the planet. The ocean,
more than any other part of our planet,...is a classic example of the
absolute need for international, global action.

Thor Heyerdahl

I pledge allegiance to the world,
To cherish every living thing,
To care for earth and sea and air,
With peace and freedom everywhere.

Lillian Genser
Women's International League for Peace and Freedom

ADDITIONS:

20
Social Justice

Peace is not just the absence of war but the presence of justice.

Anonymous

If you want peace, work for justice.   **Pope Paul VI**

Only justice ends war.   **Anonymous**

There is something within the human spirit that cries for and demands to be treated with basic fairness and justice. When such is violated, peace is undermined. Seeking justice for others is a way to peace.

Myron R. Chartier

The best defence of peace is not power, but the removal of the causes of war...

Lester B. Pearson
former Prime Minister, Canada

The simple repression of subversion can never be a lasting remedy, for it fails to take account of the causes of subversion. Most of the causes reside in our situations of institutionalized violence. Thus the radical remedy for subversion is the radical suppression of social inequalities...

Declaration of the International Meeting
of Latin American Bishops
Nonviolence: A Power for Liberation
November/December 1977

We live in a whole climate of violence. There is violence in the area of economics by reason of acute fiscal crises, the repeated devaluation of our currencies, unemployment, and soaring taxes— the burden of which ultimately falls on the poor and helpless. There is violence at the political level, as our people in varying degrees are deprived of their right of self-expression and self-determination and of the exercise of their civil rights. Still more grave in many countries are human-rights violations in the form of torture, kidnappings, and murder. Violence also makes its appearance in various forms of delinquency, in drug abuse as an escape from reality, in the mistreatment of women—all tragic expressions of frustration and of the spiritual and cultural decadence of a people losing their hope in tomorrow.

Declaration of the International Meeting
of Latin American Bishops
November/December 1977

It is organized violence on top which creates individual violence at the bottom.

Emma Goldman

There are two different sorts of violence: violence of assault and violence of defense. There are those who seek "conflict at any price" and there are those who seek "peace at any price." The price in both cases is violence....We reject both brands of violence. And we call for the radical elimination, not of the enemy, surely, but of the root cause of the enmity.

Chilean Bishops
The Gospel and Peace
September 1975

We realize conflicts may not cease. But we know that increasing the size and capabilities of the military is like increasing the size of a band-aid when a disorder is internal.

Healing will take place only as we understand and treat the root causes of instability within and between nations.

Women's Peace Presence

Peace cannot suddenly descend from the heavens. It can only come when the root-causes of trouble are removed.

Jawaharlal Nehru

...since justice is indivisible, injustice anywhere is an affront to justice everywhere.

Martin Luther King, Jr.

If a free society cannot help the many who are poor, it cannot save the few who are rich.

John F. Kennedy

We know that a peaceful world cannot long exist one-third rich and two-thirds hungry.

Jimmy Carter
1977

We cannot build a secure world upon a foundation of human misery.

Robert McNamara

Development is the new word for peace.

Anonymous

...those who defend the ideal of liberating the underdeveloped lands from the slavery of communism should learn from Paul VI that poverty also is a slavery, and that freedom is an empty word...absolutely meaningless for the two-thirds of humanity who are slaves to hunger, disease, ignorance and colonialism.

Archbishop Dom Helder Camara

...their politics are confined to bread.

Mahatma Gandhi

Poverty is the worst form of violence.   **Mahatma Gandhi**

Hunger and poverty are no accidents. They are the fruits of social injustice.

Clergy and Laity Concerned

...statistics suggest that the world hunger problem is not one of inadequate food, but one of unequal distribution of the available resources—food, sanitation, education.

Hamilton, Whitney, and Sizer
Nutrition, Concepts and Controversies

The myths that hunger results from overpopulation or insufficient production have been exploded. The planet has the productive capacity and technology to feed the population. Hunger is the product of unjust policies and economic structures, of consumerism and materialism, of greed and avarice.

Moises Sandoval

It is often argued that poverty is caused by people's having too many children, but persuasive statistics from many sources reveal that this is not the cause of their poverty. Rather, the poverty is the cause of their having so many children: hunger is one of the prime causes of the population explosion.

Hamilton, Whitney, and Sizer
Nutrition, Concepts and Controversies

There is enough food for everyone. But not everyone has enough food. Too much food produced by the poor feeds the animals eaten by the rich. Too much land in developing countries produces cash crops for the industrialized world. When some people go hungry, it is not food that's in short supply—it's justice.

Food First **newsletter**

I worked on the hacienda over there, and I would have to feed the dogs bowls of meat or bowls of milk every morning, and I could never put those on the table for my own children. When my children were ill, they died with a nod of sympathy from the landlord. But when the dogs were ill, I took them to the veterinarian in Suchitoto.

You will never understand violence or nonviolence until you understand the violence to the spirit that happens from watching your children die of malnutrition.

a peasant in El Salvador
Witness to War

Half of Central America's agricultural land produces food for export, while in several of its countries the poorest 50 percent of the population

eat only half the protein they need. (The richest 5 percent, on the other hand, consume two to three times more than they need.)
                                                    Frances Moore Lappé and J. Collins
                                                    Food First: Beyond the Myth of Scarcity

Mexico now supplies the United States with over half of its supply of several winter and early spring vegetables, while infant deaths associated with poor nutrition are common.
                                                    Frances Moore Lappé and J. Collins
                                                    Food First: Beyond the Myth of Scarcity

We see dramatic news footage of South African police shooting randomly into crowds. We hear daily reports of more deaths caused by violence. But what many people do not know is that apartheid kills in other ways. Many more black South Africans die from hunger than from police violence—some 50,000 black children die from hunger every year.
                                                    Food First newsletter

Apartheid means starvation in a land of plenty. South Africa is among the top seven food exporters in the world. Every year it exports more than a billion dollars worth of beef, grain, vegetables and fruit.
    Yet every day 136 black children die from hunger.
    The problem is not a lack of food but a lack of justice. It is apartheid—South Africa's system of racial domination—that keeps the black majority hungry. There can be no end to hunger in South Africa without an end to apartheid.
                                                    Food First newsletter

Africa is a net exporter of barley, beans, peanuts, fresh vegetables, and cattle (not to mention luxury crop exports such as coffee and cocoa), yet it has a higher incidence of protein-calorie malnutrition among young children than any other continent.
                                                    Frances Moore Lappé and J. Collins
                                                    Food First: Beyond the Myth of Scarcity

...if we compare the sums we receive from abroad in the form of investments with the money returning there, we see that we, the poor, the underdeveloped are helping the developed countries. This is shocking! It's unbelievable!
                                                    Archbishop Dom Helder Camara

The tragic scenario unfolds this way. Large landowners and multinational corporations control the best farmlands, and they use them mainly to grow crops that can be exported at considerable profit. Native persons work for below-subsistence wages and are forced onto marginal lands to do their own farming. The poor work hard, but they are cultivating crops for other people, rather than for themselves. The money they earn is not enough even to buy the products they help produce. The result is that the foods they export—bananas, beef, cocoa, coconuts, coffee, pineapples, sugar, tea, winter tomatoes, and others fill our grocery stores, while the poor who grow these foods, have even less food than before. Countless examples can be cited to illustrate how natural resources are diverted from producing food for domestic consumption to producing luxury crops for those who can afford them.

Hamilton, Whitney, and Sizer
Nutrition, Concepts and Controversies

Paying for a worldwide military presence is part of this nation's hidden cost...for relatively low-cost bananas, clothes, gasoline and aluminum foil.

Russell Herman

The primary reason for hunger in Ethiopia is that the government in power is essentially a military government, with military priorities.

Joe Collins
Institute for Food and Development Policy

Peace we want because there is another war to fight against poverty, disease and ignorance. We have promises to keep to our people of work, food, clothing and shelter, health and education.

Indira Gandhi

We must abandon our Edsel policy of building ever more devastating bombs and win the important competition to produce better lives and economies in the Third World. Americans must join to take the management of the American enterprise away from the experts who produced the Edsel.

William E. Colby
former Director, CIA

Stop looking at nations by who their leaders are allies with and start looking at leaders and how they meet the needs of their people.

Anonymous

Our nation cannot call for respect for human rights when it lacks the moral courage to save its own cities, its own poor, its own minorities whose rights are trampled upon.

Vernon Jordan

The mark of a civilized society is that people are fed and clothed and housed.

Madge Micheels-Cyrus

Someone has described this country as having socialism for the rich and capitalism for the poor.

Anonymous

The pathos of it all is that the America which is to be protected by a huge military force is not the America of the people, but that of the privileged class; the class which robs and exploits the masses, and controls their lives from the cradle to the grave.

Emma Goldman

The arms race is the welfare program of the sun belt and the upper class.

I. F. Stone

Without "industrial disarmament"—that is, an absolute reduction in global demand for raw materials and energy, and a corresponding technological transformation—it will be possible neither to attain a genuine military disarmament nor to restore the ability of poor Southern Hemisphere countries to provide themselves with adequate means of subsistence. The voracity of our giant industrial machinery cannot do without rapid deployment forces and neocolonial production branches.

Rudolf Bahro

We consume arms, we consume useless products, we consume everything in sight. And we end up by consuming human beings themselves.

Adolfo Pérez Esquivel
1980 Nobel Peace Prize
Christ in a Poncho

No one has the right to create an economy at the expense of the world's poor.

Adolfo Pérez Esquivel
1980 Nobel Peace Prize
Christ in a Poncho

* I sit on a man's back choking him and making him carry me, and yet assure myself and others that I am sorry for him and wish to lighten his load by all possible means—except by getting off his back.

Leo Tolstoy

No world settlement that affords nations only a place on relief rolls will provide the basis for a just and durable peace.

William O. Douglas

Capitalism and communism are both imperialisms that provide only half answers. They make the human being an object....We want something besides capitalism or communism, something on the order of self-management and sharing.

Adolfo Pérez Esquivel
1980 Nobel Peace Prize
Christ in a Poncho

What good is culture, philosophy, or science if men and women become objects instead of subjects?

Adolfo Pérez Esquivel
1980 Nobel Peace Prize
Christ in a Poncho

There are two ways to get enough. One is to continue to accumulate more and more. The other is to desire less.

G. K. Chesterton

Find out how much God has given you, and from it take what you need; the remainder is needed by others. The superfluities of the rich are the necessities of the poor. Those who retain what is superfluous possess the goods of others.

St. Augustine

There is an important task of education facing us, especially with our youth, lest they too be dragged into the consumer society we have created for ourselves. We must help them find life values, life's essential values. They must learn that a more just and humane world is possible only if...we live with our sisters and brothers in understanding, in sharing, and in communion.

Adolfo Pérez Esquivel
1980 Nobel Peace Prize
Christ in a Poncho

I am a man of peace. God knows how I love peace. But I hope I shall never be such a coward as to mistake oppression for peace.

Lajos Kossuth

All oppression creates a state of war.

Simone de Beauvoir

* The man who has got everything he wants is all in favour of peace and order.

Jawaharlal Nehru

Nothing is so hard for those who abound in riches as to conceive how others can be in want.

Jonathan Swift

Those who make peaceful change impossible, make violent revolution inevitable.

John F. Kennedy
Address to Latin American Ambassadors
1963

Whatever the apparent cause of any riots may be, the real one is always want of happiness. It shows that something is wrong in the system of government that injures the felicity by which society is to be preserved.

Thomas Paine
1792

* For the social revolution means nothing if it is not a battle for humanity against all that is inhuman and unworthy of man. That is why we have always asserted that the more there is of real revolution, the less there is of violence; the more violence, the less of revolution.

Barthelemy de Ligt

There can be no beauty if it is paid for by human injustice, nor truth that passes over injustice in silence, nor moral virtue that condones it.

Tadeusz Borowski
This Way for the Gas, Ladies and Gentlemen

Some things you must always be unable to bear....Injustice and outrage and dishonor and shame. No matter how young you are or how old you have got....Just refuse to bear them.

William Faulkner

They made us many promises, more than I can remember, but they never kept but one; they promised to take our land, and they took it.

Anonymous Native American

Red power means we want power over our own lives....We do not wish power over anyone. We are only half a million Indians. We simply want the power, the political and economic power, to run our own lives in our own way.

Vine Deloria
National Congress of American Indians
1966

Power should not be concentrated in the hands of so few and powerlessness in the hands of so many.

Maggie Kuhn

In South Africa:
● Blacks are 70% of the population but can own land in just 13% of the country.
● Blacks can own no more than 4 acres of land, while white farms average 3,000 acres.
● Black workers earn as little as $30 per month, and unemployment is over 25 percent.
● Blacks are denied basic rights such as voting and deciding where to live.

Institute for Food and Development Policy

Those who invest in South Africa are here for what they get out of our cheap and abundant labor. They are buttressing one of the most vicious systems.

Bishop Desmond Tutu
1984 Nobel Peace Laureate

Women constitute half the world's population, perform nearly two-thirds of its work hours, receive one-tenth of the world's income and own less than one-hundredth of the world's property.

United Nations Report
1980

Individuals can resist injustice, but only a community can do justice.

Jim Corbett
sanctuary worker

But if by some miracle, and all our struggle, the Earth is spared, only justice to every living thing (and everything is alive) will save humankind.

Alice Walker

We move from the quicksands of social injustice to the solid rock of human dignity.

Martin Luther King, Jr.

All we ask, Oh Lord, is to be safe from the rain, just warm enough in winter to watch the snow with a smile, enough to eat so that our hunger will not turn us to angry beasts, and sanity enough to make a justice that will not kill our love of life.

Joseph Pintauro

Although the world is very full of suffering, it is also full of the overcoming of it.

Helen Keller

ADDITIONS:

21
By and About the Soviets

A bad compromise is better than a good battle.

Russian proverb

In recent times a complete change has come about. Today, Russia possesses in reality, and not simply on paper, an army which is always prepared for battle and which can quickly be concentrated at a given location....We believe that the conquest of Europe [by Russia] will be easy in the future if the social order of Europe continues to deteriorate and if the governments continue to grow weaker...and particularly if France is completely debilitated politically by an increasing republicanization or by socialistic-communistic revolutions.

Baron August von Haxthausen
1852

No nation in the history of battle ever suffered more than the Soviet Union suffered in the course of the Second World War. At least 20 million lost their lives. Countless millions of homes and farms were burned or sacked. A third of the nation's territory, including nearly two-thirds of its industrial base, was turned into a wasteland—a loss equivalent to the devastation of this country east of Chicago.

John F. Kennedy
June 1963

Soviet War Deaths—WWI and WWII: 31,700,000
American War Deaths—Civil War through Vietnam: . . . 1,000,000

Defense Monitor
Center for Defense Information

They [Soviets] don't want nuclear war any more than we do. In fact, in many ways they—this generation has been through hell. They lost 20 million people. They talk to you about it all the time. They don't want to see their children go through the hell they went through. And anybody that thinks they want to bring war to their territory just doesn't understand this generation of Russian leaders.

Averell Harriman
former US Ambassador to the USSR

I find the view of the Soviet Union that prevails today in our government and journalistic establishments so extreme, so subjective, so far removed from what any sober scrutiny of external reality would reveal, that it is not only ineffective, but dangerous as a guide to political action. This endless series of distortions and over-simplifications; this systematic dehumanization of the leadership of another great country; this routine exaggeration of Moscow's military capabilities and of the supposed inequity of its intentions; this daily misrepresentation of the nature and the attitudes of another great people...this reckless application of the double standard to the judgment of Soviet conduct and our own; this failure to recognize the commonality of many of their problems and ours as we both move inexorably into the modern technological age...these, believe me, are not the marks of the maturity and realism one expects of the diplomacy of a great power.

George Kennan
former US Ambassador to the USSR

Our anti-communism has become so totally a national obsession that it colors and dominates all our thinking, all our planning, and all our name-calling. We no longer give much thought to what is better for America, but rather what is worse for Russia. The most effective argument in official debate or personal argument is the assertion that communists favor a course of action someone is opposing.

The Progressive
October 1951

The Nation which indulges toward another an habitual hatred or an habitual fondness is in some degree a slave. It is a slave to its animosity or to its affection, either of which is sufficient to lead it astray from its duty and its interest.

George Washington

* Fear of Communism has more often than not poisoned us to our roots. Fear of Communism degraded us by murdering Sacco and Vanzetti. Fear of Communism caused countless deaths and mutilations in the Labor Movement in the years before World War II. This terrible fear, inflamed by Senator Joe McCarthy, turned friend against friend, wife against husband, brother against brother and ruined the lives and reputations of hundreds of innocent men and women, thirty years ago. Most catastrophic of all, encouraged by industrial profiteers, our fear has led us into wars in places we never belonged; wars whose dismal outcome can show little or no gain, moral or physical, for the fact of our participation. Hideous and bloody stalemates like Korea, or far worse, Vietnam, where thousands and thousands died utterly futile deaths, or returned home maimed and brutalized in body and spirit.

William Styron
author, Duke University speech

We have been opposed to any social change that carried the taint of the political left, especially any change that could be labeled "communistic." We have supported fascists, dictators, and military juntas—anyone who professes "anti-communism"—no matter how oppressive and reactionary, no matter how they retard the legitimate aspirations of the people, as long as they served the perceived temporary self-interests of the United States. We have become the caretakers of the status quo.

Anti-communism is an inadequate substitute for a rational and humanitarian foreign policy; we should express a concern for people and not their ideology....The world of the "good guys and the bad guys" may be less complex, less troublesome, and problems seem to be more easily resolved, but it simply does not exist.

Dale E. Noyd
Air Force officer who refused to go to Vietnam
We Won't Go

No government or social system is so evil that its people must be considered as lacking in virtue. As Americans, we find communism profoundly repugnant as a negation of personal freedom and dignity. But we can still hail the Russian people for their many achievements....Both the United States and its allies, and the Soviet Union and its allies have a mutually deep interest in a just and genuine peace and in halting the arms race.

John F. Kennedy

We use a word like "Communist." POW! That person vanishes. We have all kinds of emotional content in that word Communist. I want you to know that I went to the Communist bloc countries to share some of our knowledge, and do you know what I found? (And don't let it get out.) They're people just like you...did you know that? They don't have tails, 'cause I looked. And they don't have horns, because I felt. But they do cry just like you do, and they do care about their kids just the way you do, and they do feel lonely sometimes and they do feel great joy sometimes and sometimes they dance in the street and sing happy songs, just like you. Isn't that incredible? "Communist." POW! Just the word alone is enough for us to get a gun and go kill 'em. The horror of words!

Leo Buscaglia

I've been called naive and stupid because I say the Russians cannot be all evil and let's go and get acquainted, but the idea of talking with Communists does not strike me with shaking palsy....Here are two populous and intelligent but poorly communicating masses of people, living far from each other, speaking different languages, seldom seeing each other, and really having nothing tangible to quarrel about, who are poised ready to attack each other.... I say, for the love of God and humanity and Earth and all the goodness—yes, and all of the sorrows— let us not deliberately continue carelessly this eye-for-an-eye and tooth-for-a-tooth behavior.

Dr. Karl Menninger

If we insist on demonizing these Soviet leaders—on viewing them as total and incorrigible enemies, consumed only with their fear or hatred of us and dedicated to nothing other than our destruction—that, in the end, is the way we shall assuredly have them, if for no other reason than that our view of them allows for nothing else, either for us or for them.

George Kennan
former US Ambassador to the USSR

Psychologists tell us that we always project our most loathsome and vile features onto the enemy.

Rusty Schweickart
Apollo Astronaut

I'd like to have a world with peace because I could make friends with the Russian people and have even more friends than what I have now.

6th Grader

Many fear that we cannot work with the Russians. The truth is that we already are doing so.   **William Ury**

The problems presented by the Soviet Union are serious. But stereotypes do not provide us with an adequate basis for responding intelligently.

Marshall D. Shulman
former State Department employee

Americans should know the people of the Soviet Union—their hopes and fears and the facts of their lives...people-to-people initiatives...will help break down stereotypes, build friendships, and, frankly, provide alternatives to propaganda.

Ronald Reagan
November 1985

One superpower is noted for its advocacy of "political" human rights, the other for its attention to "economic" human rights—yet both blocs are notorious for rights they neglect or ignore.

International Fellowship of Reconciliation

Human Rights! New York is where you should look for violations. There, the people have to sleep on the sidewalks and sift through garbage cans.

Andrei Gromyko
May 1984

Either we have to learn to live with the Russians or we and the Russians will die at about the same time. And I am all for living.

George Kistiakowsky
scientist, Manhattan Project

The Soviet Union is not our enemy, nuclear weapons are the enemy. We're going to have to learn to live with the Russians or we and the Russians are going to die at about the same time.

Rear Admiral Gene R. La Rocque
U.S. Navy (retired)

The communist threat grows strong when there are prospects for weapons contracts but diminishes as opportunities to market American goods in Russia present themselves.   **Robert Aldridge**

Unfortunately, we've tended to think of arms control as being some sort of favor that we're doing for the Soviet Union. So when the Soviet Union misbehaves, we cancel the arms control negotiations. That makes no sense.

Paul Warnke
U.S. negotiator for SALT II

The Soviet buildup is not a sudden surge. It has been a long-range program. I don't necessarily think that buildup is for adventures around the world. It is my feeling that they are doing it because they feel it is necessary for their own security.

Gerald Ford
January 1977

The Soviets learn their lessons well, but in many cases too well, and they may find themselves doomed to repeat history by paying too much attention to it. Virtually every major characteristic of the Soviet groundforce structure and every attendant tactic is a result of a lesson learned (usually at great cost) during World War II.

Edward A. Miller
Assistant Secretary of the Army for Research and Development
and Lt. General Howard H. Cooksey
Deputy Army Chief of Staff for
Research, Development, and Acquisition

The Soviets are upgrading and expanding the ballistic missile defense system at Moscow but are thus far remaining within the limits of the treaty.

General John A. Wickham, Jr.
Army Chief of Staff
on Soviet Anti-Ballistic Missile Treaty compliance
1984

The 100-missile interceptor defense projected for the ongoing Moscow upgrade would quickly be exhausted in a large-scale attack....The available evidence does not indicate with any certainty whether the Soviets are making preparations for deployments beyond the limits of the ABM Treaty.

General Charles A. Gabriel
Air Force Chief of Staff
1984

As you know, with the subs and missiles, they have pretty well conformed to SALT II. There may have been some cheating on the margins, but they have pretty well stuck to the numbers requirements in SALT I and II, and we can see that as they dismantle their subs and whatnot.

General Charles A. Gabriel

New missiles, bombers and aircraft carriers are being churned out in some kind of pathological obsession. The present U.S. Administration is thinking in terms of war and acting accordingly.

Andrei Gromyko
January 1984

Militarism, hostility and war hysteria are exported together with those missiles. As a result, the world is pushed closer and closer to a nuclear abyss.

Dmitri Ustinov
March 1984

There are some who would like to turn space into an arena of aggression and war, as is clear from the plans announced in the United States.

Konstantin Chernenko
May 1984

It is a long time since the American capital has seen such a noisy militaristic orgy, arranged by the Reagan Administration on the occasion of the burial of the Unknown Soldier.

TASS (Soviet press agency)
May 1984

[The Reagan Administration] has chosen terrorism as a method of conducting affairs with other states and peoples.

Konstantin Chernenko
June 1984

The Americans and the Soviets are literally scaring each other to death...

George McGovern
August 1985

We must make sure that we don't allow ourselves to get involved in a lot of senseless competition with the West over military spending....We must be prepared to strike back against our enemy, but we must also ask, "Where is the end of this spiraling competition?"

Nikita Khrushchev

There is no illusion more dangerous than the idea that nuclear war can still serve as an instrument of policy, that one can attain political aims by using nuclear weapons and at the same time get off scot-free oneself, or that acceptable forms of nuclear war can be found.

N. A. Talenski
Soviet Major General

The first time one of those things is fired in anger, everything is lost. The warring nations would never be able to put matters back together.

Leonid Brezhnev

Above all, nuclear powers must avert those confrontations which bring an adversary to a choice of either a humiliating retreat or a nuclear war. To adopt that kind of course would be evidence only of the bankruptcy of our policy—or a collective death wish for the world.

John F. Kennedy

In a nuclear war, the survivors would envy the dead.

Nikita Khrushchev

Today, when the danger is looming large, when several minutes is enough for millions of people in any part of the planet to get annihilated in a nuclear conflagration, we must rally still closer the ranks of those who struggle for peace, against the threat of a nuclear catastrophe, so as to preserve life on Earth, and save our children's future.

Using concerted efforts, we should seek to make the new negotiations between our countries to be held on questions of nuclear and outer space armaments, constructive, just, and having as their basis the principle of equality and equal security.

K. Proskurnikova
Vice-President
Soviet Women's Committee
January 1985

* When you reach America again…tell them that here we are full of joy and love, we are not afraid. Tell them that our life, the life of the church, is a miracle. Tell them that the Church is alive. We can see and feel here the presence of the kingdom of God, and tell them that we must pray for each other, and for the peace of the whole world.

Mrs. Voskrenenia
Russian hostess for visiting American Christians

Better to turn back than lose your way.

Russian proverb

ADDITIONS:

(See also quotes in Chapter 2—Facts of the Arms Race—especially page 23 by Dimitri Ustinov.)

22
Spirituality of Peace

A. Inner Peace
B. Love
C. Moral Condemnation of Violence and War
D. Spiritual Teachings
E. The Bible on Peace
    1. The Old Testament
    2. The New Testament
F. Religion and Politics

What we have experienced and are still experiencing must surely convince us that the spirit is everything and that institutions count for very little....The best planned improvements in the organization of our society cannot help us at all until we have become at the same time capable of imparting a new spirit to our age.

Albert Schweitzer
The Decay and Restoration of Civilization
1923

* I do not believe the greatest threat to our future is from bombs or guided missiles. I don't think our civilization will die that way. I think it will die when we no longer care—when the spiritual forces that make us wish to be right and noble die in the hearts of men. Arnold Toynbee has pointed out that 19 of 21 civilizations have died from within and not conquest from without. There were no bands playing and flags waving when these civilizations decayed. It happened slowly, in the quiet and the dark when no one was aware.

Lawrence Gould
former President
Carleton College

* With the phenomenal rise and spread of Western civilization we have now become the richest materialistic nation that ever existed on this planet, and we have created untold benefits for all mankind. The monstrous paradox is that we have impoverished ourselves spiritually in the process.

Frank Waters
The American Indian Speaks

* You white men will soon be crushed under your machines, rotting in the endless swamp of your materialism. You have lost the essence of man; the impulse toward something that is more than yourselves.

Nikos Kazantzakis

* Admittedly it may take an all-out fatal shock treatment, close to catastrophe, to break the hold of civilized man's chronic psychosis. Even such a belated awakening would be a miracle. But with the diagnosis so grave and the prognosis so unfavorable, one must fall back on miracles— above all, the miracle of life itself, that past master of the unexpected, the unpredictable, the all-but-impossible.

Lewis Mumford
The Origins of War

People usually consider walking on water or in thin air a miracle. But I think the real miracle is not to walk either on water or in thin air, but to walk on earth.

Thich Nhat Hanh

* The world needs a revolution in feeling, in sensitivity, in orientation, in the spirit of man.

A. J. Muste

A. Inner Peace

There never was a war that was not inward; I must fight till I have conquered in myself what causes war...

Marianne Moore

...your ideas form your private and mass reality. You want to examine the universe from the outside, to examine your societies from the outside. You still think that the interior world is somehow symbolic and the exterior world is real. That wars, for example, are fought by themselves or with bombs. All of the time, the psychological reality is the primary one, that forms all of your events.   (Seth) Jane Roberts
The Individual and the Nature of Mass Events

When we do not find peace within ourselves, it is vain to seek for it elsewhere.

Duc François de La Rochefoucauld

He had so much security inside that he could afford to go without any outside.

said about Kagawa, a Japanese pacifist
Courage in Both Hands

To me the only answer to all our problems, whether they're political, economic, personal or whatever, is to act from the center of ourselves. Act, not react. Acting from the wholeness that we are, which is our soul level...and when we contact that we're not defensive or on the defensive or offensive or anything else because we're secure in what we are. We know who we are. We know we're part of the whole.

Dorothy Maclean
founder of Findhorn

I make myself rich by making my wants few.

Henry David Thoreau

B. Love

* Free love? As if love is anything but free! Man has bought brains, but all the millions in the world have failed to buy love. Man has subdued bodies, but all the power on earth has been unable to subdue love. Man has conquered whole nations, but his armies could not conquer love.

Emma Goldman

We believe the spiritual force capable of both changing us and stopping the arms race is that of *agape*: the love of God operating in the human heart.

Jim Douglass
Sojourners
February 1984

Love, as revealed and interpreted in the life and death of Jesus Christ, involves more than we have yet seen, and is the only power by which evil can be overthrown and the only sufficient basis for human society.

International Fellowship of Reconciliation

Peace is the work of justice indirectly, in so far as justice removes the obstacles to peace; but it is the work of charity (love) directly, since charity, according to its very notion, causes peace.

Thomas Aquinas
Summa Theologica

All the good that you will do will come not from you but from the fact that you have allowed yourself, in the obedience of faith, to be used by God's love. Think of this more and gradually you will be free from the need to prove yourself, and you can be more open to the power that will work through you without your knowing it.

Thomas Merton

Love alone is capable of uniting living beings in such a way as to complete and fulfill them, for it alone takes them and joins them by what is deepest in themselves.

Teilhard de Chardin

Conspire, in its literal sense, means "to breathe together." Pierre Teilhard de Chardin urged "a conspiracy of love."

Marilyn Ferguson
The Aquarian Conspiracy

* Fear, a more or less reflexive response that we share with other species, drives each of us, as an individual, to save himself in the face of danger. Fear cannot distinguish between a fire in one's own house and a nuclear holocaust—between one's own death and the end of the world—and is therefore useless even to begin to suggest to us the meaning of the nuclear peril. Its meaning can be grasped only to the extent that we feel the precise opposite of fear, which is a sense of responsibility, or devotion, or love, for other people, including those who have not yet been born. In Germany, the Peace movement has inverted the traditional Biblical admonition "Fear not" to say "You must fear." But the original version was the right one, for nuclear matters as for others. Fear isolates. Love

connects. Only insofar as the latter is strong in us are we likely to find the resolve to prevent our extinction.

Jonathan Schell

The only real security in the end is the love we have given and the love we have received.

Friends Journal, May 1980

"Cogito, ergo sum," said Descartes. "I think, therefore I am." Nonsense! Amo, ergo sum—I love, therefore I am.

William Sloane Coffin

...to love human beings is still the only thing worth living for...without that love, you really do not live.

Søren Kierkegaard

The ultimate miracle of love is this...that love is given to us to give to one another.

Anonymous

...it is not how much we do, but how much love we put in the action that we do.

Mother Teresa
Nobel Peace Prize Speech

All works of love are works of peace.

Mother Teresa

(See also Chapter 23, **Nonviolence**—pages 161–180)

C. Moral Condemnation of Violence and War

* I saw prevailing throughout the Christian world a license in making war of which even barbarous nations would have been ashamed; recourse was had to arms for slight reason or for no reason; and when arms were once taken up, all reverence for divine and human law was thrown away; just as if all men were thence forth authorized to commit crimes without restraint.

Hugo Grotius
1625

There is perhaps no phenomenon which conveys so much destructive feeling as moral indignation, which permits envy or hate to be acted out under the guise of virtue.

Erich Fromm

Christian values are never defended by murder, torture, or repression. Sad indeed would be those "humanistic, Christian values" that require violence for their maintenance.

**Declaration of the International
Meeting of Latin American Bishops
November/December 1977**

War is the greatest plague that can afflict humanity; it destroys religion, it destroys states, it destroys families. Any scourge is preferable to it.

Martin Luther

War and preparation for war must be judged in moral perspective, perspective derived from centuries of collective experience and expressed in our great religious traditions. These traditions agree with striking similarity and clarity that we must neither contemplate nor prepare for the killing of innocent persons. The killing of innocent people is an inevitable characteristic of warfare. The rejection of war is the conclusion of morality seriously applied to politics.

Fellowship of Reconciliation

[When warfare] involves such an extension of evil that it entirely escapes from human control, its use must be rejected as immoral....The pure and simple annihilation of all human life is not permitted for any reason whatsoever.

Pope Pius XII

The God of peace is never glorified by human violence.

Thomas Merton

Nothing can be politically right, that is morally wrong; and no necessity can ever sanctify a law, that is contrary to equity.

**Benjamin Rush
1786**

Our sole safeguard against the very real danger of a reversion to barbarianism is the kind of morality which compels the individual conscience, be the group right or wrong. The individual conscience against the atom bomb? Yes. There is no other way.

Life
August 1945

Sensitivity to the immense needs of humanity brings with it a spontaneous rejection of the arms race, which is incompatible with the all out struggle against hunger, sickness, under- development and illiteracy.

Pope John Paul II

We as concerned citizens recognize...Billions are being spent on arms, while people's basic needs, such as food, housing, health care and education are underfunded, that to be able to kill and to be killed many times over in the name of defense is an evil waste of world resources.

United Church of Christ
Reversing the Arms Race
a Pronouncement of the General Synod 12
1979

The armaments race...is to be condemned unreservedly. Even when motivated by a concern for legitimate defense, it is in fact...an injustice. The obvious contradiction between the waste involved in the overproduction of military devices and the extent of unsatisfied vital needs...is in itself an act of aggression against those who are victims of it. It is an act of aggression which amounts to a crime, for even when they are not used, by their costs alone armaments kill the poor by causing them to starve.

Vatican statement
to the United Nations on Disarmament
1976

As Christians we believe that armaments and military force are inconsistent with the ways of Jesus Christ and the biblical hope of justice and peace.

American Baptist Churches
Resolution on Disarmament
adopted by the General Board
1978

The nuclear arms race may well be regarded as the penultimate subject of our time. There is no greater affront to the Lord and Giver of life, no more convincing evidence of human enslavement to the dark powers of this age, and no more urgent cause for the church's prophetic witness and action....The nuclear arms race is first and foremost a false religion. It is, to be sure, also bad politics, bad economics, bad science, and bad war. It can and should be opposed on all these fronts.

Reformed Church in America
Christian Faith and the Nuclear Arms Race: A Reformed Perspective
1980

The use of the modern technology of war is the most striking example of corporate sin and the prostitution of God's gifts.

Church of England Bishops
1978

...In every age God's people have identified sin and called its servants to repentance. Now it is our turn. It is not good enough to condemn only the sins which everyone agrees are evil and uncivil. We will have to see the idolatry of our time and identify the false god of nuclear weaponry. To topple this idol may leave our neighbors, both within and without the church, feeling momentarily insecure and afraid. But with the death grip of a false security weakened, they may find true hope in the Giver of Life....We believe that the concept of nuclear deterrence, which involves a trust in nuclear weapons, is a form of idolatry.

Mennonite Central Committee
1978

The taproot of violence in our society today is our intention to use nuclear weapons. Once we have agreed to that, all other evil is minor in comparison. Until we squarely face the question of our consent to use nuclear weapons, any hope of large scale improvement of public morality is doomed to failure.

Richard McSorley

In a recent radio broadcast Mr. Reagan urged that schools include the teaching of morality in the classroom along with content. The present moment, then, appears to be the appropriate time to discuss the morality of war, the morality of stockpiling nuclear weapons, and the morality of peace since these are among the greatest issues of our times.

Grandmothers For Peace Newsletter
Fall 1985

* Nuclear war is politically irrational and morally an indefensible and hideous atrocity, whoever perpetrates it. Preparation for such war is also politically irrational, and since there is no guarantee that the preparation will lead to anything but war, the preparation itself is an atrocity and a degradation of mankind.

A. J. Muste

It's a sin to build a nuclear weapon.

Richard McSorley

Even the possession of weapons which cannot be morally used is wrong. They are a threat to peace and might even be the cause of nuclear war. The nuclear weapons of communists may destroy our bodies. But our intent to use nuclear weapons destroys our souls. Our possession of them is a proximate occasion of sin.

Richard McSorley

Nuclear weapons aren't weapons—they're an obscenity.

Dr. Marvin Goldberger
President
California Institute of Technology

All the missiles that ELF can trigger are centered on the heart of Christ.

Michael Miles
Poppy Seed Six

God made heaven and earth in 7 days and the bomb can ruin it all in two seconds. That isn't fair to God.

Rachel M.
Baltimore
Age 6
Please Save My World

* We are now living in the shadow of an arms race more intense, more costly, more widespread and more dangerous than the world has ever known. Never before has the human race been as close as it is now to total self-destruction. Today's arms race is an unparalleled waste of human and material resources; it threatens to turn the whole world into an armed camp; it aids repression and violates human rights; it promotes violence and insecurity in place of the security in whose name it is undertaken; it frustrates humanity's aspirations for justice and peace; it has no part in God's design for His world; it is demonic.

World Council of Churches
Conference on Disarmament
April 1978

D. Spiritual Teachings on Peacemaking

Peace is more than the absence of war, more than a precarious balance of powers. Peace is the intended order of the world with life abundant for all God's children.

United Presbyterian Church in the USA
General Assembly, 1980

* The Great Spirit who has made us all has given us different complexions and different customs. Why may we not conclude that he has given us different religions, according to our understanding?

Red Jacket
Seneca Indian
1792

I have given you lands to hunt in,
I have given you streams to fish in,
I have given you bear and bison,
I have given you roe and reindeer,
I have given you brant and beaver,
Filled the marshes full of wild fowl,
Filled the rivers full of fishes;
Why then are you not contented?
Why then will you hunt each other?

Gitche Manitou in
Song of Hiawatha
Henry Wadsworth Longfellow

* Our fathers came to this western area to establish a base from which to carry the gospel of peace to the people of the earth. It is ironic, and a denial of the very essence of that gospel, that in this same general area there should be constructed a mammoth weapons system potentially capable of destroying much of civilization.

The Church of Jesus Christ of Latter-Day Saints (Mormons)
on the MX missile
1981

We express profound concern about the danger of a precarious balancing of humanity on the brink of nuclear catastrophe. We know that still more terrible weapons are being developed which can only lead to greater fear and suspicion and thus to a still more feverish arms race. Against this we say with one voice—NO! In the name of God, NO!...Thus the Lord has set before us again life and death, blessing and curse: Therefore, choose life that you and your descendants may live.

Christ is Our Peace
joint communiqué issued by the Metropolitan Juvenaly
(Russian Orthodox Church)
and Dr. Claire Randall
National Council of Churches
1980

Biblical imperatives call us to fie to our idolatrous sense of security in the arms race, our profiteering in weapons of death, and our infatuation with violence, and to become alive to the good news of peace, the ministry of reconciliation, the way of suffering love, and resurrection faith in the Kingdom coming.

New Call to Peacemaking
Second National Conference
1980

Only by moving with the Tao, or the Way, or the will of God, can we hope to bring peace on earth.

Anonymous

From Taoism we learn that religion is a mode of connectedness with the creative force of life. When one is thus connected one's actions are responsive to the needs of life; when one is truly part of the body of humankind, then a hurt in one part of the body will trigger remedial action in the other parts.

Anonymous

Lord, make me an instrument of Your peace; where there is hatred, let me sow love; where there is injury, pardon; where there is discord, union;

where there is doubt, faith; where there is despair, hope; where there is darkness, light; and where there is sadness, joy.

O Divine Master, grant that I may not so much seek to be consoled as to console, to be understood as to understand, to be loved as to love; for it is in giving that we receive, it is in pardoning that we are pardoned, and it is in dying that we are born to eternal life.

St. Francis of Assisi

We find our security in God, not in weapons, and would point those around us to that security.

Church of the Brethren
resolution adopted at the Annual Conference
1980

* We humans are not misbegotten progeny, children of the curse. We need not rape and kill—one another, mother earth, earthly father, anyone. Born as we are, helpless, vulnerable, weaponless, we need not become subjects of the new biology of violence....We are the disarmed daughters and sons of a disarmed God, who in Christ, bares Himself, body and blood, to deterrent powers of this world. And so disarms death itself.

Daniel Berrigan

The servants of the All-Merciful are those who go about the earth with gentleness, and when the foolish ones address them, they answer, "Peace!"

Koran 25:63

O humankind! Behold We created you male and female and We made you into nations and tribes so that you might come to know one another.

Koran 49:13

If you are not for you who will be? If you are only for you what's the purpose?

Rabbi Hillel

...the truest and greatest power is the strength of Peace...because Peace is the Will of the Great Spirit...

Hopi Declaration of Peace

...we've got to admit—it feels good, when someone has wronged us, to "get 'em back." If they've done wrong to someone—they should have a taste of their own medicine. Right? Fair is fair.

It makes sense to me...but not...to my Lord.

According to Matthew and Luke, Jesus said: "You have heard it was said: An eye for an eye, and a tooth for a tooth. But now I tell you—do not take revenge on someone who wrongs you. If someone slaps you on the right cheek, let them slap you on the left as well."

Lynn S. Larson

An eye for an eye. A Hiroshima for a Pearl Harbor. A Hanoi for a Saigon. A contra-force for a revolution. Twelve executions in Florida and Texas for twelve murders in Florida and Texas. A warhead for a warhead. An El Salvador for an Afghanistan. A cussing out for a costly mistake. A rude look for a cold shoulder.

An eye for an eye and a tooth for a tooth: We've learned it too well!

Jesus said: "You've heard an eye for an eye and a tooth for a tooth...but I'll tell you a better way."

Lynn S. Larson

There is no rigid distinction between peace among nations, economic justice, bodily health and a spiritually right relationship with God.

Wes Granberg-Michaelson
Reformed Church in America

Peace is not simply the absence of war, a nuclear stalemate or combination of uneasy cease-fires. It is that emerging dynamic reality envisioned by prophets where spears and swords give way to implements of peace (Isaiah 2:1–4); where historic antagonists dwell together in trust (Isaiah 11:4–11); and where righteousness and justice prevail. There will be no peace with justice until unselfish and informed love are structured into political processes and international arrangements.

The United Methodist Church and Peace
adopted by the General Conference
1980

We spoke of our oneness in Christ with Russian believers and the fragile bridge that our churches are building between East and West. We promised to remain as one with our Russian sisters and brothers in Christ, no matter what our governments may do.

As we spoke, we saw human faces like our own—heads nodding in assent, eyes filled with tears, smiles of hope. Then we walked through the congregation. Hands reached out to touch us. And the people greeted us in Russian with words that have a deeper meaning for us now: "Christ is risen!" and "Peace!"

Robert White
A Holiday in the Soviet Union

Peacemaking is fundamentally a spiritual struggle, a battle for the soul of humanity.

Richard Barnet
a founder of World Peacemakers

E. The Bible on Peace
1. The Old Testament

Thou shalt not kill.

Exodus 20:13
King James Version

...you shall demolish their altars, smash their sacred pillars and cut down their sacred poles. You shall not prostrate yourselves to any other god.

Exodus 34:13
The New English Bible

I have set before you life and death, blessing and curse; therefore choose life, that you and your descendants may live...

Deuteronomy 30:19
Revised Standard Version

Do you want long life and happiness?...strive for peace with all your heart.

Psalm 34:12,14
Today's English Version

* How beautiful upon the mountains are the feet of him who brings good tidings, who publishes peace...

Isaiah 52:7
RSV

Take away from me the noise of your songs; to the melody of your harps I will not listen. But let justice roll down like waters, and righteousness like an ever-flowing stream.

Amos 5:23–24
RSV

(See also Chapter 29—Visions of Peace—pages 261–275.)

2. The New Testament

> The teachings of Christ are becoming subversive again—as they were in the days of the Roman Empire.
>
> I. F. Stone

Blessed are the peacemakers: for they shall be called the children of God.

Matthew 5:9
KJV

* You have heard that it was said, "An eye for an eye, and a tooth for a tooth." But now I tell you: do not take revenge on someone who wrongs you. If anyone slaps you on the right cheek, let him slap your left cheek too.

Matthew 5:38
TEV

You have heard that it was said, "Love your friends, hate your enemies." But now I tell you: love your enemies and pray for those who persecute you...

Matthew 5:43
TEV

* What good will it be for a man if he gains the whole world, yet forfeits his soul?

Matthew 16:26a
New International Version

* Glory to God in the highest, and on earth peace, good will toward men.

Luke 2:14
KJV

Would that even today you knew the things that make for peace.

Luke 19:42
RSV

Let us therefore follow after the things which make for peace...

Romans 14:19
KJV

* Be not deceived; God is not mocked: for whatsoever a man soweth, that shall he also reap.   **Galatians 6:7**
KJV

But the wisdom from above is pure, first of all; it is also peaceful, gentle, and friendly; it is full of compassion and produces a harvest of good deeds; it is free from prejudice and hypocrisy. And goodness is the harvest that is produced from the seeds the peacemakers plant in peace.

James 3:17, 18
TEV

There is no fear in love; perfect love drives out all fear.

1 John 4:18a
TEV

* If someone says, "I love God," but hates his brother, he is a liar. For he cannot love God, whom he has not seen, if he does not love his brother, whom he has seen. This, then, is the command that Christ gave us: he who loves God must love his brother also.   **1 John 4:20,21**
TEV

F. Religion and Politics

To see the universal and all-pervading Spirit of Truth face to face, one must be able to love the meanest creature as oneself. Whoever aspires after that cannot keep out of any field of life...those who say that religion has nothing to do with politics do not know what religion means.

Mahatma Gandhi

* The straightforward course, and the one that would serve the Church best in the long run, would be to close our professedly Christian Churches the moment war is declared by us, and reopen them only on the signing of the treaty of peace. No doubt to many of us the privation thus imposed would be far worse than the privation of the prosaic inconveniences of war. But would it be worse than the privation of faith, and the horror of the soul, wrought by the spectacle of nations praying to their common Father to assist them in blowing one another to pieces with explosives that are also corrosives, and of the Church organizing this monstrous paradox instead of protesting against it?

George Bernard Shaw

If all the Churches of Europe closed their doors until the drums ceased rolling they would act as a most powerful reminder that though the glory of war is a famous and ancient glory, it is not the final glory of God.

George Bernard Shaw
Common Sense about the War
1914

The biblical insight that violence against others imperils our relationship to all creation finds a startling expression in the nuclear threat....Abolishing nuclear weapons, eliminating hunger and saving the ozone layer are all part of a biblical call to earthkeeping, and should be addressed by the church not as individual political issues, but as indivisible dimensions of our response to God's love.

Wes Granberg-Michaelson
Reformed Church in America

* As Christians we recognize a demonic element in the complexity of our world, but we also affirm our belief in the good will and purpose and Providence of God for his whole creation. This requires us to work for a world characterized not by fear, but by mutual trust and justice.

Episcopal Church
Christian Attitudes to War in a Nuclear Age
1981

The present insanity of the global arms race, if continued, will lead inevitably to a conflagration so great that Auschwitz will seem like a minor rehearsal....The nuclear issue is not just a political issue—it is a

moral and spiritual issue as well.... I believe that the Christian especially
has a responsibility to work for peace in our world....We must seek the
good of the whole human race, and not just the good of any one nation
or race.

Billy Graham

...for it is God and God alone who is justified in using the credo "Peace
Through Strength."

Peter Monkres

The church that bows before the altar of national pride and militarism
leaves the gospel there.

Mernie King
Sojourners Fellowship

From the vantage point of history, we can view the churches of the past
and accuse them of social and political captivity. They are easy enough
to recognize. Our favorites are the German national church that bowed
before Nazism and deserted its Lord for a new lord, and the white church
of the South that worshipped at the altars of racial superiority and forgot
its Lord. What can be said of the captivity of an American church that
has for 30 years largely supported a government that plans nuclear war?

Mernie King
Sojourners Fellowship

* We must win clear of the tendency to associate religion and spirituality
with withdrawal from the world and the field of action. The Goddess is
ourselves *and* the world—to link with Her is to engage actively with the
world and all its problems.

Starhawk
The Spiral Dance

ADDITIONS:

23
Nonviolence

The natives were good people, for when they saw I would not remain, they supposed I was afraid of their bows and arrows, and taking the arrows they broke them into pieces and threw them into the fire.

Henry Hudson
of the people he found along the river later named for him
1609

* A good end cannot sanctify evil means; nor must we ever do evil, that good may come of it. We are too ready to retaliate, rather than forgive or gain by love and information....Force may subdue, but love gains. And he that forgives first, wins the laurel.

William Penn

There is no greater fallacy than the belief that aims and purposes are one thing, while methods and tactics are another.

Emma Goldman

The means is the end in the process of becoming.

Jacques Maritain
Catholic philosopher

The means are the seeds that bud into flower and come to fruition. The fruit will always be of the nature of the seed planted.

19th century American pacifist

All who affirm the use of violence admit it is only a means to achieve justice and peace. But peace and justice *are* nonviolence...the final end of history. Those who abandon nonviolence have no sense of history. Rather they are bypassing history, freezing history, betraying history.

André Trocmé

The method of nonviolent resistance is effective in that it has a way of disarming opponents. It exposes their moral defenses, weakens their morale and at the same time works on their conscience. It makes it possible for the individual to struggle for moral ends through moral means.

Martin Luther King, Jr.

If one takes care of the means, the end will take care of itself....We have always control over the means and never of the ends.

Mahatma Gandhi

His fundamental trust was that the most effective way of defending those for whom he was responsible was to keep on using the right means.

speaking of Ned Richards
Courage in Both Hands

You will understand, if you are a practicing idealist, that you cannot kill in the name of peace. For if you do so your methods will automatically undermine your ideal. The sacredness of life and spirit are one and the same....The end does not justify the means. If you learn that lesson, then your good intent will allow you to act effectively and creatively in your private experience and in your relationships with others. Your changed beliefs will affect the mental atmosphere of your nation and of the world.

(Seth) Jane Roberts
The Individual and the Nature of Mass Events

If it were proved to me that in making war, my ideal had a chance of being realized, I would still say "No" to war. For one does not create a *human society* on mounds of corpses.

Louis Lecoin
French pacifist leader

I would say that I'm a nonviolent soldier. In place of weapons of violence, you have to use your mind, your heart, your sense of humor, every faculty available to you...because no one has the right to take the life of another human being.

Joan Baez

* If we kill man, with whom are we to live?

Thich Nhat Hanh
Vietnamese pacifist

I shall die, but that is all that I shall do for Death.

Edna St. Vincent Millay
Wine from These Grapes

I am prepared to die but there is no cause for which I am prepared to kill.

Mahatma Gandhi

* The greatest heroes of the world are not men who kill other men in war. They are quiet heroes who are brave in other ways.

Rufus Jones
Quaker

Patriotism is not enough, I must have no hatred or bitterness for anyone.

Edith Cavell
nurse killed by German firing squad during WWI

Don't ever let them pull you down so low as to hate them.

Booker T. Washington

Hate is too great a burden to share.

Martin Luther King, Jr.

Hatred is like rain in the desert—it is of no use to anybody.
African saying

The price of hating other human beings is loving oneself less.
Eldridge Cleaver

* Hatred, which could destroy so much, never failed to destroy the man who hated and this is an immutable law.
James Baldwin

Anger is an acid that can do more harm to the vessel in which it stands than to anything on which it's poured.
Anonymous

When you clench your fist, no one can put anything in your hand, nor can your hand pick up anything.
Alex Haley
Roots

...we cannot sow seeds with clenched fists. To sow we must open our hands.
Adolfo Pérez Esquivel
1980 Nobel Peace Prize
Christ in a Poncho

Interior presence—cannot occupy the human soul at the same time that it is occupied by hatred.
Ann Fairbairn
Five Smooth Stones

We must find an alternative to violence. The eye-for-an-eye philosophy leaves everybody blind.
Martin Luther King, Jr.

An eye for an eye and a tooth for a tooth—that way everyone in the world will soon be blind and toothless.
Fiddler on the Roof

Imagine the vanity of thinking that your enemy can do you more damage than your enmity.
St. Augustine

Never in the world can hatred be stilled by hatred; it will be stilled only by non-hatred—this is the law eternal.
Buddha

Christ knew also, just as all reasonable human beings must know, that the employment of violence is incompatible with love, which is the fundamental law of life.

Leo Tolstoy
September 1910

We know too that one evil cannot be cured by another. Evils don't cancel each other out. They total up.

Adolfo Pérez Esquivel
1980 Nobel Peace Prize
Christ in a Poncho

The ultimate weakness of violence is that it is a descending spiral, begetting the very thing it seeks to destroy. Instead of diminishing evil, it multiplies it. Through violence you murder the hater, but you do not murder hate. In fact, violence merely increases hate....Returning violence for violence multiplies violence, adding deeper darkness to a night already devoid of stars. Darkness cannot drive out darkness; only light can do that.

Martin Luther King, Jr.

We must meet hate with creative love.   **Martin Luther King, Jr.**

Hatred and bitterness can never cure the disease of fear, only love can do that. Hatred paralyzes life; love releases it. Hatred confuses life; love harmonizes it. Hatred darkens life; love illumines it.

Martin Luther King, Jr.

Our truth is an ancient one: that love endures and overcomes; that hatred destroys; that what is obtained by love is retained, but what is obtained by hatred proves a burden.

American Friends Service Committee
Speak Truth to Power

Many waters cannot quench love, neither can the floods drown it.

Song of Solomon

If a single person achieves the highest kind of love it will be sufficient to neutralize the hate of millions.

Mahatma Gandhi

Only one individual is necessary to spread the leavening influence of *ahimsa* [non-violence] in an office, school, institution or country.

Mahatma Gandhi

Love is the most durable power in the world....Love is the only force capable of transforming an enemy into a friend.

Martin Luther King, Jr.

When the power of love overcomes the love of power, then there will be true peace.

Sri Chin Moi Gosh

* ...there is only one thing that has power completely, and that is love; because when a man loves he seeks no power, and therefore he has power.

Alan Paton
Cry, the Beloved Country

* Military power is as corrupting to the man who possesses it as it is pitiless to its victims. It is just as devastating to its employer as it is to those who suffer under it.

American Friends Service Committee
Speak Truth to Power

Power in our society is seen as "power over" and that's an addictive drug that you have to keep taking over and over again. It doesn't last. You have to continue to dominate other people in order to still feel powerful.

If you feel proud of who you are and strong with who you are, then you realize there is not a scarcity of power; that if one person has power then another person can have it also, can have their power....That's sharing of power.

Geof Morgan

The theory and practice of nonviolence are roughly at the same stage of development today as those of electricity in the early days of Marconi and Edison.

David Dellinger

Nonviolence is a mighty opportunity for Christians today and all men and women of goodwill. Now they have a way to strike a blow for a society whose goal will be victory over all forms of domination.

Declaration of the International Meeting of Latin American Bishops November/December 1977

In nonviolence, the masses have a weapon which enables a child, a woman, or even a decrepit old man to resist the mightiest government successfully. If your spirit is strong, mere lack of physical strength ceases to be a handicap.

Mahatma Gandhi

No longer can any liberation movement anywhere in the world truly claim that "revolutionary" violence is the only path open to them to effect change. For the overthrow of Marcos, like the overthrow of the former Shah of Iran, shows without question that even late in the twentieth century, it is still possible for an unarmed but mobilized population to overthrow a conscienceless, technologically sophisticated, dictatorial regime, backed by the most powerful military power in the history of the world, through recourse to the tactics and strategies of *nonviolent action*.

David H. Albert
People Power: Applying Nonviolence Theory

* First, it must be emphasized that nonviolent resistance is not a method for cowards; it does resist. If one uses this method because he is afraid or merely because he lacks the instruments of violence, he is not truly nonviolent.

Martin Luther King, Jr.

Practice nonviolence not because of weakness, practice nonviolence being conscious of strength and power; no training in arms is required for realization of strength.

Mahatma Gandhi

There is nothing so strong as gentleness; nothing so gentle as real strength.

Anonymous

[In response to then-President Marcos' continued attacks on her lack of political experience] I concede that I cannot match Mr. Marcos when it comes to experience. I admit that I have no experience in cheating, stealing, lying or assassinating political opponents.

Corazon Aquino
Time, February 3, 1986

Gandhi once declared that it was his wife who unwittingly taught him the effectiveness of nonviolence. Who better than women should know that battles can be won without resort to physical strength? Who better than we should know all the power that resides in noncooperation?

Barbara Deming
Revolution and Equilibrium

World peace through nonviolent means is neither absurd nor unattainable. All other methods have failed. Thus we must begin anew.

Martin Luther King, Jr.

The choice is no longer between violence and nonviolence. It is between nonviolence and nonexistence.

Martin Luther King, Jr.

* For perhaps the first time in history reflective men have had to grapple with the pacifists' question: "Can national interests and human values really be served by waging a war with atomic and hydrogen weapons?"

James Reston
New York Times column

Some of you will ask a further question: If we abandon reliance upon military force—before international agreements have been signed—upon what alternative power can our country rely? The answer, I would say, is clearly the power of nonviolent resistance.

Barbara Deming
Revolution and Equilibrium

There is no escape from the impending doom save through a bold unconditional acceptance of the nonviolent method. Democracy and violence go ill together. The states that today are nominally democratic have either to become frankly totalitarian or, if they are to become truly democratic, they must become courageously nonviolent.

Mahatma Gandhi

No sovereign people defending its land can be subjugated from without. If a people is destroyed, it first destroys itself from within. It becomes flaccid, loses contact with the land, which is turned into property, and with its own powers, which are delegated to the state. It becomes, in short, like the peoples of nuclear-bearing powers, who are not only at the mercy of their weapons, but so sapped in strength and resolve that they can scarcely imagine an alternative to them. If a modern nation, by contrast, ever became accomplished in non-violence, it could resist an aggressor without weaponry and through active non-cooperation and other means of non-violent resistance.

Joel Kovel

The abolition of war does not require anti-war, anti-military lobbies or demonstrations and protest, but the development of effective nonviolent alternatives to military struggle.

Gene Sharp

The only effective defense at this point in history is social defense—the organized nonviolent resistance of a whole population to an invader.

former West German General Gerd Bastian
1983

In dozens and hundreds of significant conflicts, including international ones...nonviolent struggle has already taken the place of military violence.

Gene Sharp

...in nonviolent combat what we do is just exactly what nice players aren't supposed to do. We refuse to play by one of the rules the system tries to foist on us: the rule that says you have to counter violence with violence. If your opponents can get you to swallow that idea, then they can unleash still greater violence on you. The essential thing in nonviolent combat is for us to render these tactics inoperative by refusing to play by the rules and by imposing our own conditions instead.

Adolfo Pérez Esquivel
1980 Nobel Peace Prize
Christ in a Poncho

You can make tyranny helpless by refusing cooperation with it.

Gene Sharp

...if, as revolutionaries, we will wage battle without violence, we can remain very much more in control—of our own selves, of the responses to us which our adversaries make, of the battle as it proceeds and of the future we hope will issue from it.

Barbara Deming

Nonviolent resistance is the only type of defense which, from beginning to end, yields to the enemy not even a prospect of any of the usual rewards of invasion: prestige, glory, indemnity, subject people, trade or military advantages, available territory, triumph of ideas.

Jesse Wallace Hughan
1942

First, something seems wrong to most people engaged in struggle when they see more people hurt on their own side than on the other side. They are used to reading this as an indication of defeat, and a complete mental readjustment is required of them....Vengeance is not the point; change is.

Barbara Deming
Revolution and Equilibrium

Victory can be achieved by various means. It can be gained with tanks and missiles, but I think that one wins better with truth, honesty and logic....This is a new weapon.

Lech Walesa
November 1982

...Nonviolence is a weapon fabricated of love. It is a sword that heals. Our nonviolent direct action program has as its objective not the creation of tensions, but the surfacing of tensions already present. We set out to precipitate a crisis situation that must open the door to negotiation. I am not afraid of the words "crisis" and "tension." I deeply oppose violence, but constructive crisis and tension are necessary for growth. Innate in all life, and all growth, is tension. Only in death is there an absence of tension.

Martin Luther King, Jr.

Non-violent direct action seeks to create such a crisis and establish such creative tension that a community that has constantly refused to negotiate is forced to confront the issue.

Martin Luther King, Jr.

Conflict there will still be between one nation, one class, one group, and another. Let those who have faith in the justice of their cause demonstrate their conviction by self-suffering, not by attempting to coerce or to destroy the "enemy."

Mahatma Gandhi

* Nonviolence is the answer to the crucial political and moral questions of our time; the need for man to overcome oppression and violence without resorting to oppression and violence.

  Man must evolve for all human conflict a method which rejects revenge, aggression and retaliation. The foundation of such a method is love.

Martin Luther King, Jr.

I believe that unarmed truth and unconditional love will have the final word in reality. That is why right, temporarily defeated, is stronger than evil triumphant.

Martin Luther King, Jr.

Nonviolence is not a garment to be put on and off at will. Its seat is in the heart, and it must be an inseparable part of our being.

Mahatma Gandhi

Nonviolence, which is a quality of the heart, cannot come by an appeal to the brain.

Mahatma Gandhi

Nonviolence is a plant of slow growth. It grows imperceptibly, but surely.

Mahatma Gandhi

* All I claim is that every experiment of mine has deepened my faith in nonviolence as the greatest force at the disposal of mankind.

Mahatma Gandhi

Resistance and nonviolence are not in themselves good. There is another element in our struggle that then makes our resistance and nonviolence truly meaningful. That element is reconciliation. The tactics of nonviolence without the spirit of nonviolence may become a new kind of violence.

Martin Luther King, Jr.

* Nonviolence means avoiding not only external physical violence but also internal violence of spirit. You not only refuse to shoot a man, but you refuse to hate him.   **Martin Luther King, Jr.**

We should be innocent not only of violence but of all enmity, however slight, for it is the mystery of peace.

St. John Chrysostom

Peacemaking aims at transformation and reconciliation. We are engaged in transforming relations. We are not seeking to make people accept the results of a long history of enmity but rather to recognize enmity, to discover its causes, to find the human face beneath the enemy image, and to struggle with every gift we have to heal division and brokenness.

Jim Forest
International Fellowship of Reconciliation

Satyagraha was a term I coined because I did not like the term "passive resistance"....Its root meaning is "holding on to truth," hence "force of righteousness." I have also called it love force or soul force....the mighty power of truth to be set against the evil of falsehood.

Mahatma Gandhi

We try to act in truth. This is what gives our movement its security: the truth—respect for the human person. Respect for the human person generates constancy and steadfastness. And constancy and steadfastness generate an attack on evil and the possibility of altering the structures of injustice.

Adolfo Pérez Esquivel
1980 Nobel Peace Prize
Christ in a Poncho

Once people understand the strength of nonviolence—the force it generates, the love it creates, the response it brings from the total community—they will not easily abandon it.

Cesar Chavez

Nonviolence is the constant awareness of the dignity and humanity of oneself and others; it seeks truth and justice; it renounces violence both in method and in attitude; it is a courageous acceptance of active love and goodwill as the instrument with which to overcome evil and transform both oneself and others. It is the willingness to undergo suffering rather than inflict it. It excludes retaliation and flight.

Wally Nelson
conscientious objector and tax resister

Nobody was born nonviolent. No one was born charitable. None of us comes to these things by nature but only by conversion. The first duty of the nonviolent community is helping its members work upon themselves and come to conversion.

Lanza del Vasto

The nonviolent revolution begins in your mind. You must first redefine yourself. When people redefine themselves, slavery is dead. Then the power structure makes a motion, but doesn't get a second.

James Bevel

The first step toward liberation occurs when a human being comes aware that he or she is a person.

Adolfo Pérez Esquivel
1980 Nobel Peace Prize
Christ in a Poncho

...The important thing is to awaken a critical consciousness in the basic communities, so they can find their own solutions to their problems.

Adolfo Pérez Esquivel
1980 Nobel Peace Prize
Christ in a Poncho

The basic community has some unique characteristics: It enables each member to find himself or herself as a person. It develops a sense of solidarity, a sense of a community of brothers and sisters....Here is a mighty force for changing the structures of injustice that mark our society.

Adolfo Pérez Esquivel
1980 Nobel Peace Prize
Christ in a Poncho

Be what you want to become. Thus, if you want to have free elections, begin by freely electing someone; if you want to have free speech, speak freely; if you want to have a trade union, found a trade union. The Poles discovered that if enough people act in this way, the very foundation of the unwanted government begins to dissolve even while it retains the monopoly on the means of violence.

Solidarność

But nonviolent defense requires not only willingness to risk one's life (as any good soldier, rich or poor, will do). It requires renunciation of all claims to special privileges and power at the expense of other people.

David Dellinger

The major advances in nonviolence have not come from people who have approached nonviolence as an end in itself, but from persons who were passionately striving to free themselves from social injustice.

David Dellinger

The first thing to be disrupted by our commitment to nonviolence will be not the system but our own lives.

Jim Douglass

To change the world for the better you must begin by changing your own life. There is no other way. You begin by accepting your own worth as a part of the universe and by granting every other being that same recognition. You begin by honoring life in all of its forms. You begin by changing your thoughts toward your contemporaries, your country, your family, your working companions. If the ideal of loving your neighbor like yourself seems remote, you will at least absolutely refrain from killing your neighbor. And your neighbor is any other person on the face of the planet. You cannot love your neighbor, in fact, until you love yourself, and if you believe that it is wrong to love yourself, then you are indeed unable to love anyone else.

(Seth) Jane Roberts
The Individual and the Nature of Mass Events

For a start you will acknowledge your existence in the framework of nature, and to do that you must recognize the vast cooperative processes that connect each species with each other one. If you truly use your prerogatives as an individual in your country, then you can exert far more power in normal daily living than you do now. Every time you affirm the rightness of your own existence, you help others. Your mental states are part of the planet's psychic atmosphere.

(Seth) Jane Roberts

Hopefully you will see...as something of your mission, a mission of peace and prosperity...a mission of love—of love that not only extends to one's enemies. You know, I've had a lot of experience loving my enemies—I've been thrown in jail and beaten up and I never lost my temper with the Ku Klux Klan. The problem is that I have lost my temper with my wife, I have lost my temper with my mother, I have lost my temper with my 12-year-old son—but ultimately the problems that we talk about on a macroeconomic level or on a global level, all come back to that human level where we begin to learn to love one another at home, and in families and in one-to-one relationships; where we begin to appreciate those differences, where we begin to develop partnerships...

Andrew Young
Boston College commencement speech
June 1985

...nonviolent actions are by their nature androgynous. In them the two impulses that have long been treated as distinct, "masculine" and "feminine," the impulse of self assertion and the impulse of sympathy, are clearly joined; the very genius of nonviolence, in fact, is that it demonstrates them to be indivisible....One asserts one's rights as a human being, but...asserts them...as rights belonging to another person.

Barbara Deming
Two Perspectives on Women's Struggle

* The nonviolent approach does not immediately change the heart of the oppressor. It first does something to the hearts and souls of those committed to it. It gives them new self-respect; it calls up resources of strength and courage that they did not know they had. Finally, it reaches

the opponent and so stirs his conscience that reconciliation becomes a reality.

Martin Luther King, Jr.

As long as people accept exploitation, exploiter and exploited will be entangled in injustice. But once the exploited refuses to accept the relationship, refuses to cooperate with it, they are already free.

Mahatma Gandhi

A nonviolent person will not oppress another person; nor will they be oppressed.

Madge Micheels-Cyrus

A liberation movement that is nonviolent sets the oppressor free as well as the oppressed.

Barbara Deming

The question isn't who is the enemy, but what is the enemy?

American Friends Service Committee
Speak Truth to Power

One must never confuse error with the person that errs.

Pope John XXIII

Let's show the world we know a way to grow, inwardly as human beings. Let's show them how they can win a fight without hatred or underhandedness. A person can grow as a human being by defending truth or justice. A person can grow as a human being by learning to distinguish between people and their acts.

The "Snarlers" of the Perús Cement Company
Brazil, 1974
Christ in a Poncho

* Nonviolence is a method of achieving change. Nonviolent action is a way of confronting someone who's responsible for a wrong with the facts of his evil and the respect for his personhood.

American Friends Service Committee
Speak Truth to Power

Many oppressors are also oppressed. Nonviolent confrontation is the only confrontation that allows us to respond realistically to such complexity.

Jane Meyerding
Reclaiming Nonviolence

Nonviolence has the unique ability to simultaneously accept and reject— to acknowledge and connect us with that which is valuable in a person at the same time as it resists and challenges that person's oppressive attitude or behavior.

Jane Meyerding
Reclaiming Nonviolence

* Passive resistance is an all-sided sword, it can be used anyhow; it blesses him who uses it and him against whom it is used.

Mahatma Gandhi

* It has always been a mystery to me how men can feel themselves honoured by the humiliation of their fellow beings.

Mahatma Gandhi

I always prefer to believe the best of everybody—it saves so much trouble.

Rudyard Kipling

* We have to remember that God loves all men, that God wills all men to be saved, that all men are brothers. We must love the jailor as well as the one in prison. We must do that seemingly utterly impossible thing: love our enemy.

Dorothy Day

Help me to know that my love's not complete until I have loved the oppressor.

Lee Domann
from the song "Peace with Justice"

* Heretic, rebel, a thing to flout,
They drew a circle that shut him out.
But love and I had the wit to win,
We drew a circle that took them in.

Edwin Markham

---

* Senator: Mr. President, I believe that enemies should be destroyed.
President Lincoln: I agree with you sir, and the best way to destroy an enemy is to make him a friend.

Truth has given me the trail of peace, honoring all, fearing none.

Eddie Benton-Banai

We will match your capacity to inflict suffering with our capacity to endure suffering. We will meet your physical force with soul force. We will not hate you, but we cannot in good conscience obey your unjust laws....And in winning our freedom, we will win you in the process.

Martin Luther King, Jr.

If you want to see the brave, look at those who can forgive. If you want to see the heroic, look at those who can love in return for hatred.

from the Bhagavad Gita

It can't be measured on the Richter Scale, but can you fathom the power of the words from the cross: "Forgive them...they know not what they do."

Lynn S. Larson

Those who discovered the law of nonviolence in the midst of violence were greater geniuses than Newton.

Mahatma Gandhi

Nonviolence is really tough. You don't practice nonviolence by attending conferences—you practice it on the picket lines.

Cesar Chavez

I knew someone had to take the first step and I made up my mind not to move.

Rosa Parks
refused to move to the back of the bus
Montgomery, Alabama
December 1955

Yes, the challenge of those who believe in nonviolent struggle is to learn to be aggressive enough.

Barbara Deming

Nonviolence doesn't always work—but violence never does.

Madge Micheels-Cyrus

Violence is rejection as well as attack, a denial of needs, a reduction of persons to the status of objects, to be broken, manipulated or ignored. Violence is any human act or social process that deprives, debases, or exploits people. Violence is any sword that diminishes people by dividing them from one another, from themselves, from what they have made, from what they can become, from the world around them.

American Friends Service Committee

Violence leaves society in monologue rather than dialogue.

Martin Luther King, Jr.

Violence is resourcelessness.

Jo Vellacott
Women, Peace and Power

I love my country with my conscience. It would be a sort of treason to use arms to defend what is so precious.

Philippe Vernier
French pastor, WWII

The "peace" won by violence proves only to be a pause between wars, with each war more disastrous than the one before.

International Fellowship of Reconciliation

We have always questioned armed liberation movements—for today's oppressed will become tomorrow's oppressors.

Adolfo Pérez Esquivel
1980 Nobel Peace Prize
Christ in a Poncho

I despair to see so many radicals turn to violence as a proof of their militancy and commitment. It is heart-breaking to see all the old mistakes being made all over again. The usual pattern seems to be that people give nonviolence two weeks to solve their problem...and then decide it has "failed." Then they go on with violence for the next hundred years...and it seems never to "fail" and be rejected.

Ted Roszak

Once the connection between conflict and violence is broken, it can be a very creative experience.

Thomas Fehsenfeld

Nonviolence offers no guarantees. But the curious thing is that people who do violence don't receive any guarantees either. Statistics show that you have a better chance of coming out alive in a nonviolent battle.

Joan Baez

Violent changes are, in effect, limited to the sphere of technology. They are simply power shifts or power reversals which cannot even pretend to attempt the abolition of hierarchical (i.e., oppressive) practices. Violence can be an effective method for reform, but it cannot effect radical change.

Jane Meyerding
Reclaiming Nonviolence

I do not believe in violence...hatred...or armed insurrection. They take place too quickly. They change the circumstances of people's lives without giving them time to adapt to the changes. It is useless to dream of reforming socio-economic structures...without a corresponding deep change in our inner lives.

Archbishop Dom Helder Camara

...it is absurd to talk of revolution without nonviolence, because all violence is reactionary, causing the exact conditions it intends to destroy.

Ira Sandperl

A violent revolution is no revolution at all. It only perpetuates the old conditions.

James Bevel

There is a contradiction in the term "violent revolutionary" because revolution means change, and violence is a reversion to a former pattern.

Joan Baez

Nonviolence is the most revolutionary method for social change.

Anonymous

The only thing that's been a worse flop than the organization of nonviolence has been the organization of violence.

Joan Baez

* I think also that deep down somewhere in me, and in all men at all times, there is a realization that the pattern of violence meeting violence makes no sense, and that war violates something central in the human heart— "that of God" as we Quakers sometimes say.

Albert Bigelow

In the evolution of civilization, if it is to survive, all men and women cannot fail eventually to adopt Gandhi's belief that the process of mass applications of force to resolve contentious issues is fundamentally not only wrong, but contains within itself the germs of self-destruction.

General Douglas MacArthur

What makes the neglect of this particular idea [that worldwide knowledge of nonviolent tactics could avert bloodshed] so odd is that most people, if they are asked, say that they don't much believe in killing. It's not bloodlust that perpetuates violence so much as a lack of imagination, an unwillingness to reconsider. As a result, most of us specialize in rebutting new ideas so that we can quickly forget about them.

**The New Yorker
December 1983**

* But when I note the reluctance with which men today go to war even when obviously hostile armies and navies are arrayed against them and they naturally believe that if they do not kill they will be killed, I find no good reason for supposing that any army could be gotten to invade a people which flatly renounced war.

A. J. Muste

The pen is mightier than the sword.

Edward Robert Bulwer-Lytton
Governor-General of India
1875-1880

An army of principles will penetrate where an army of soldiers cannot.

Thomas Paine
1795

No army can withstand the strength of an idea whose time has come.

Victor Hugo

An invasion of armies can be resisted; an invasion of ideas cannot be resisted.

Victor Hugo
1877

There is one thing stronger than all the armies in the world, and that is an idea whose time has come.

The Nation
April 1943

No force is as great as an idea whose time has come.

Pierre Teilhard de Chardin

Suddenly knowledge and wisdom from our social and behavioral sciences is coalescing into a whole new field of nonviolent conflict management...and there is new hope.

Milton C. Mapes, Jr.
former Executive Director
National Peace Academy Campaign

ADDITIONS:

ADDITIONS:

24
Civil Disobedience

Resist much. Obey little.

Walt Whitman

It is through disobedience that progress is made.

Oscar Wilde

* I'd say that civil disobedience is...based on the idea that you break small laws—like defying lunchcounter segregation laws, or antistrike laws, or laws about draft files, or nineteenth-century laws forbidding you to shelter runaway slaves—to point out the existence of higher laws, like the brotherhood of man or the atrocity of war, which society seems to have forgotten about.

Francine Du Plessix Gray
March 1971

* Laws and conditions that tend to debase human personality—a God-given force—be they brought about by the State or individuals, must be relentlessly opposed in the spirit of defiance shown by St. Peter when he said to the rulers of his day: "Shall we obey God or man?"

Chief Albert Luthuli

* If civil authorities legislate for or allow anything that is contrary to the will of God, neither the laws made nor the authorizations granted can be binding on the consciences of the citizens, since God has more right to be obeyed than men.

Pope John XXIII

* Must the citizen even for a moment, or in the last degree, resign his conscience to the legislator? Why has every man a conscience, then? I think that we should be men first, and subjects afterward. It is not desirable to cultivate a respect for law, so much as for the right. The only obligation I have a right to assume, is to do at any time what I think right.

Henry David Thoreau
On the Duty of Civil Disobedience

Noncooperation in military matters should be an essential moral principle for all true scientists.

Albert Einstein

* The mass of men serve the state...not as men, mainly, but as machines, with their bodies....A very few—as heroes, patriots, martyrs, reformers in the great sense, and *men*—serve the state with their consciences also, and so necessarily resist it for the most part; and they are commonly treated as enemies by it.

Henry David Thoreau
On Civil Disobedience
1849

Disobedience to be civil, must be sincere, respectful, restrained, never defiant, must be based upon some well-understood principle, must not be capricious, and above all, must have no ill-will or hatred behind it.

Mahatma Gandhi

First, never kill,
Second, never hurt,
Third, commit yourself incessantly and with perseverance,
Fourth, remain always united,
Fifth, disobey the orders of the authorities that violate or destroy us.

Principles of the peasants of Alagamar, Brazil
in their nonviolent land struggle

In a society which exalts property rights above human rights, it is sometimes necessary to damage or destroy property, both because property has no intrinsic value except insofar as it contributes to human welfare, and also in order to challenge people to discover a new sense of priorities.

David Dellinger
Revolutionary Nonviolence

I came to this act because of moral imperatives. This so-called property [a missile silo] has no right to exist because it is violent and imposes indiscriminate destruction. We are in an historic moment of drastic confrontational policy in our government and economic system. No serious efforts have been made to contain this madness, much less to dismantle it. We keep making more missiles and warheads every day for greater stockpiles.

Some of us cannot stand by and let this happen without shouting and acting, "Not in my name."

Father Paul Kabat

...the United States is signatory to...the Nuremberg Principles, which outlaw weaponry of mass and indiscriminate destruction, as well as preparing for using those weapons. I come to ELF to dismantle a small portion of the nuclear death machine in the hope that this will be but a small part of the growing race amongst the peoples of the Earth to personally and collectively disarm directly, with our own hands, this illegal and immoral global oven under construction.

Tom Hastings
cut down an Extra-Low Frequency communications (ELF) pole
May 1985

It is time to make a stand for sanity, to be responsible and accountable. I choose life and I choose to go on record in that position.

Tom Hastings

The risks are great. The risks I take today are puny compared to the risks we take collectively in allowing this madness to continue unchecked.

Tom Hastings
May 1985

And so I act today in accordance with the teachings of the great spiritual teachers in history—Gandhi, Christ, the Indians—and in accordance with the basic moral underpinnings of humanity as expressed in the various world religions....These teachings find expression in various international laws to which the United States is a party—most notably the Nuremberg principles and the various Hague and Geneva Conventions. All speak of the basic respect for all life and of our responsibility to protect all life from harm. In order to fulfill this responsibility, I act here today to begin the disarming of Wisconsin ELF.

Jeff Leys
on notching an ELF pole
August 1985

Our primary duty and responsibility is to the children—to create a safe and secure future for them. I dedicate this action to those children who constantly remind me of this and who are a source of great strength to me.

Jeff Leys

As I ponder over the punishment to be meted out to these two people who were attempting to unbuild weapons of mass destruction, we must ask ourselves:...Why are we so fascinated by a power so great that we cannot comprehend its magnitude? What is so sacred about a bomb, so romantic about a missile?

...The anomaly of this situation here...is that I am called upon to punish two individuals who are charged with having caused damage to the property of a corporation in the amount of $33,000. It is this self-same corporation which only a few months ago was before me, accused of having wrongfully embezzled from the United States Government the sum of $3.6 million.

It is also difficult for me to equate the sentence I here give you for destroying $33,000 worth of property, because you have been charged—with those who stole $3.6 million worth of property but were not charged, demoted or in any way punished.

My duty is done, my conscience is clear.

U.S. District Judge Miles Lord
on sentencing two protesters to six months' probation
for damaging computer components at Sperry Corp.
November 1984

...our primary goal was to call attention to the idolatrous militarism and artifacts of our present-day society, our modern "golden calf" located in the fields, the hills, the valleys of our Mother Earth.

Father Carl Kabat

Your honor, I am the mother of three children, and it's my understanding that the parenthood of every generation, from the day the earth began, carries its responsibilities. And I believe that the responsibilities of parenthood change from generation to generation, as our world changes.

And I truly believe, deep down in my heart, that one of the responsibilities this generation has is to protect our children from the fear of holocaust....I have three children...and I don't want them to burn to death, like the children of Hiroshima....It was for that reason that I blockaded.

> **Barbara Bannon**
> **blocked entrance to the**
> **Livermore National Weapons Lab**
> **June 1983**

* Under a government which imprisons any unjustly, the true place for a just man is also a prison.

> **Henry David Thoreau**

I do not feel I stand here today as a criminal. I feel this court is dealing in trivia by making this charge against us, while those who are the real criminals (those who deal in our deaths) continue their conspiracy against humankind.

> **Greenham Common woman's statement**
> **Magistrate's Court—Newbury, England**
> **April 1982**

I still maintain hope for acquittal—slim as it is, I still have that hope. What is life worth after all if we don't have faith and hope in our brothers and sisters to act for Justice, for Peace, for Truth?

And if it should be a "guilty" verdict? I'll joyfully continue my witness wherever I'm sent in the prison system and continue to celebrate life. The government may do whatever it pleases with our bodies, but it can't touch our spirits!

> **Jeff Leys**
> **written from jail while awaiting trial**
> **September 1985**

I disagree with those who think that "doing time" is necessarily wasting time...[we can compromise] our basic beliefs or so restrict our activities that we have, in effect, imprisoned ourselves out of prison.

> **Dave Dellinger**
> *Revolutionary Nonviolence*

I may be arrested. I may be tried and thrown into jail, but I will never be silent.

> **Emma Goldman**

By our refusal to cooperate, we keep reminding them of our dissent, refusing to allow them the godlike sense that their will alone exists.
Barbara Deming

Your Honor, that's the problem with these people. They keep coming back!
the prosecutor in the Trident Nein case

* ...to compel a man to furnish contributions of money for the propagation of opinions he disbelieves and abhors, is sinful and tyrannical.
Thomas Jefferson
Virginia bill for Establishing Religious Freedom
1779

* If a thousand men were not to pay their tax bill this year, that would not be as violent and bloody a measure as it would be to pay them and enable the State to commit violence and shed innocent blood.
Henry David Thoreau

Ralph: What are you doing in jail?
Henry: What are you doing out of jail?
Ralph Waldo Emerson to Thoreau
while imprisoned for refusal to pay taxes for the Mexican War

Conscription

The most distasteful task of all for the objector to war conscription is to object. One does not live to become an objector but to create a society where such disagreeable conduct will not be necessary.
Evan Thomas
Conscience in Action

1. Historical Opposition

* A free government with an uncontrolled power for military conscription is the most ridiculous and abominable contradiction and nonsense that ever entered into the head of man. Where is it written in the Constitution, in what article or section is it contained, that you may take children from their parents and parents from their children, and compel them to fight the battle in any war in which the folly or wickedness of the government may engage itself.
Daniel Webster
1812

Much as I dislike to believe it, yet I am convinced that most of the propaganda in favor of selective conscription is founded not so much upon a desire to win the war as it is to accustom the people to this method of raising armies and thereby to establish it as a permanent system in this country. Let us not pay Prussian militarism, which we are seeking to destroy, the compliment of adopting the most hateful and baneful of its institutions.

Carl Hayden
Arizona Congressperson
1917

The claim that the draft is democratic, is the very antithesis of the truth. The draft is not democratic, it is autocratic; it is not republican, it is despotic; it is not American, it is Prussian. Its essential feature is that of involuntary servitude.

James A. Reed
Senator, Missouri
1917

Opposition to compulsory military service is characteristic of every government fit to be called a democracy....Democracies abhor that principle of compulsory service, the exercise of which menaces and may destroy their liberties....We are now told that compulsory military service is democratic. Mr. President, that is a libel and a reproach upon the name of democracy. It is as repugnant to democracy as any despotic principle which can be conceived.

Charles F. Thomas
Senator, Colorado
1917

* All our history gives confirmation to the view that liberty of conscience has a moral and social value which makes it worthy of preservation at the hands of the state. So deep is its significance and vital, indeed, is it to the integrity of man's moral and spiritual nature that nothing short of the self-preservation of the state should warrant its violation; and it may well be questioned whether the state which preserves its life by a settled policy of violation of the conscience of the individual will not in fact ultimately lose it by the process.

future Chief Justice Harlan F. Stone
The Conscientious Objector
1919

I regard the vote upon the pending measure to be the most important vote I shall ever be called upon to cast in this body. Upon the result of this vote hinges the ultimate destiny of this Republic. The question, plainly and bluntly put, is simply this: Shall we abandon the time-honored traditions of a peace-loving, liberty-loving people for that of a military despotism? That is the question in a nutshell.

Senator Billow
South Dakota
on the return of conscription, 1940

I believe that...in this bill...we are asked to vote on the adoption of compulsory selective military training and service as a permanent policy for the United States of America and to do it under the impulsion of an "emergency."

Jerry Voorhis
California Congressperson
1940

It is said that a compulsory draft is a democratic system. I deny that it has anything to do with democracy. It is neither democratic nor undemocratic. It is far more typical of totalitarian nations than of democratic nations. The theory behind it leads directly to totalitarianism. It is absolutely opposed to the principles of individual liberty which have always been considered a part of American democracy.

Robert Taft
Senator, Ohio
1948

The great mass of 18-year-olds...are given no choice. Thus...the older generation immolates the younger, on the altar of Moloch. What God, centuries ago, forbade Abraham to do even to his own son,—"Lay not thy hand upon the lad, neither do thou anything unto him"—this we do by decree to the entire youth of a nation.

A. J. Muste
Of Holy Disobedience
1952

I believe that conscription is good for our country—It's a great teacher of democracy.

Colonel Daniel O. Omer
Deputy Director
Selective Service
1967

Ultimately we should end the draft. Except for brief periods during the Civil War and World War I, conscription was foreign to the American experience until the 1940s.

Richard Nixon
1969

---

2. Vietnam Resisters

I knew I had arrived at conscientious objection. I was opposed in body and soul to the organized, budgeted, and officially sanctified use of violence called war. I was opposed to the compulsory and regimented aberration from the laws of God and reason, called conscription. I could no longer, in conscience, bear arms.

Stephen Fortunato, Jr.
while a U.S. marine
We Won't Go

I came to conscientious objection over a somewhat circuitous route—via the Marine Corps....With all the passion and exuberance of youth I became a trained killer. I went to classes where I learned how to rip a man's jugular vein out with my teeth. I growled like a tiger when I was told to growl like a tiger.

I was told that the Ten Commandments, however worthy they might be in civilian life, had to be suspended in the name of national interest. I was greatly impressed to see that an act perpetrated by the enemy was *ipso facto* vicious and deceitful, whereas the self-same act perpetrated by the United States was just and praiseworthy.

Stephen Fortunato, Jr.
We Won't Go

I am possibly confronted with fighting in a war that I believe to be unjust, immoral, and which makes a mockery of both our Constitution and the Charter of the United Nations—and the human values which they represent.

Apart from the moral and ethical issues and speaking only from the point of view of the super-patriot, it is a stupid war and pernicious to the self-interest of the United States....Although I am cognizant that an open society may have its disadvantages in an ideological war with a totalitarian system, I do not believe that the best defense of our freedoms is an emulation of that system.

Dale E. Noyd
Air Force Officer
refused to serve in Vietnam
became a Conscientious Objector after 11 years of honorable service
We Won't Go

* I think the Army does make an effort to deaden—to kill a man's sensitivities and make of him a conditioned response. Identity is destroyed effectively at basic training and patterns are drilled in hour after hour. No mind is called for, no thought process cultivated. Just do, do, do—to learn to do without thought—and, as the need arises, without resistance. It power-houses its way over any urge to resist, and when it destroys a man's natural tendency to resist when pushed, it has a soldier.

James M. Taylor
resisted while in Army
served two years of a three-year sentence
We Won't Go

* The best soldier, the Armed Forces teach us—contrary to our Christian tradition of values—is the most efficient murderer. The feeble voice of humanity's "Thou shalt not kill," is drowned out by the sergeant's roaring "Thou shalt kill and kill well!"

  "All men are brothers," we learn in our Sunday Schools. But the Army teaches, "The best soldier is the one who makes the clearest distinction between the 'good guys' [and 'bad guys']." The best soldier realizes soonest that all men are brothers except the "Japs," the "Krauts," the "Commies," the "VC."

  The best soldier ignores religion, God, and his conscience and learns to "follow orders." The best soldier can kill without thinking twice about it because he realizes that it is "his job" to do so.

  These are the values that our society has decided to instill into the minds, hearts and reflexes of its youth. These are the values that I must reject. These are the values that are contrary to the "national interest." This is why draft resistance is work in "the national interest," and in the interest of all humanity.

  Richard Boardman
  letter to the Selective Service
  gave up Conscientious Objection deferment to be a resister
  April 1967

* One would think (from the human perspective) that our society would demand that its young men should show cause why they *can* become soldiers—and if need be, to kill—in all good conscience. Instead, from the military perspective of our society, we insist that a young man must show cause why he should be allowed *to refuse* to kill, to refuse to participate in the Army.

  Richard Boardman
  letter to the Selective Service
  April 1967

* I have tried my best to arrange a compromise—only to discover that by compromising my adherence to very basic, human, ethical principles—I defeat myself and do a disservice to mankind's best interests.

  Richard Boardman
  letter to the Selective Service
  April 1967

* A truly free man would not support a totalitarian system to defend freedom;…No, I came to believe that a free man preserves his freedom by acting freely and not by following those who would herd men into regiments or send people scurrying like moles into bomb shelters. Most important of all, the free man must remain free not to kill or to support killing.

  Stephen Fortunato, Jr.
  We Won't Go

3. Draft Registration

The word "registration" to young people is code for "draft," an idea that evokes painful memories of Vietnam for many and an idea that has always seemed alien in a democratic society.

Ronald Reagan
1980 Campaign

* Registration cannot be separated from a draft; it's all part of the same program. The peacetime draft is more characteristic of a totalitarian system than a free society...[a] system of involuntary servitude. If we had not had the draft, we would never have been at war for the length of time we were in Vietnam. As long as each President had that unlimited supply of manpower, he could sustain that policy without a Congressional declaration of war.

Mark Hatfield
Senator, Oregon

To refuse military service when the time has come for it to be necessary, is to act after the time to combat the evil has run out.

Mahatma Gandhi

Though growing unemployment figures represent a major problem, they may act to improve our recruiting and retention [in the armed forces].

Secretary of Defense Harold Brown
June 1980

It all revolves around unemployment, you know, the economic thing. You know, it is ironic that most of the brothers I met in the army were in the infantry, in combat units, you know—the ones who would be doing the fighting and dying. Most of them, I found out, were just like myself, they didn't have any money, jobs were tight and they had to survive, so they joined the Army. And then— BANG—Vietnam....I noticed that most of the brothers who did go into the jungle returned to walk around in a kind of mindless stare. They did not know what they were doing out there, they did not want to go back out there, but most importantly they really began to realize, that for the most part, their commanding officers, and the army itself, considered them expendable. Racism was rampant in Vietnam. My advice to black people, or any people of color, is to stay out of the military.

Al Ceasar
Black Vietnam-era Veteran

When the time comes for you to march against the draft, think of me in this wheel chair. I thought I was fighting for the American dream. I

know now I was cheated and tricked and lost three-fourths of my body
for nothing [in Vietnam]. Now, the audacity, the madness, they want
to brutalize another generation. Well, I say if they try to bring back the
draft, they'll reap a rebellion like they've never seen.

Ron Kovic
paralyzed from the chest down
at an anti-draft rally on the Capitol steps, April 1979

Registering for the draft is like lining up for Kool Aid in Jonestown.

Daniel Ellsberg

We will not cooperate with military registration...noncooperation is the
best way to demonstrate our opposition to the return of the draft and
militarism....We do not take this position lightly. Prison, exile or the
underground is hell, but war is worse.

Rick Stryker and Mark Furman

There is no purpose for registration and a draft except as a machinery
to make interventionist wars possible abroad. Those of us who lived
through the horror of Vietnam and the abuses of the draft that made it
possible, know the hard choices ahead for America's young people.
Those choices last time split a nation, jailed thousands, sent hundreds
of thousands into exile or underground, separated families and ruined
lives, disrupted and destroyed the promise of a generation.

Central Committee on Conscientious Objection (CCCO)

The revival of draft registration is being used to threaten war....Refusing
the call to arms is based on the fundamental moral reality that there is
no longer any threat greater than war itself....The members of Sojourners
Fellowship have determined to refuse the call to arms at every point,
including registration for the draft. Further, we advocate that others
likewise refuse. Specifically, we encourage young men and women to
refuse to register for the draft and support them in that decision.

Jim Wallis
***Sojourners*, March 1980**

Registration for a military draft is a major step toward war...as leaders
of religious and academic communities...we oppose registration and will
work to stop it. We believe that many young men (and women) will
refuse to register....Some of us will resist the draft by wearing arm bands
during any registration, by picketing places of registration, or by refusing
to pay federal taxes for the draft...we hope to share some of the terrible
burden put upon our young people by a compulsory registration and draft
system that threatens once again to send them to far parts of the world
to kill and be killed.

Call to Conscience
signed by key religious and academic leaders
issued by the Fellowship of Reconciliation, April 1980

The National Resistance Committee is confident that a strategy of concerted resistance can bring conscription to a halt. The draft, like all forms of tyranny, depends on the compliance of people who become victims through their tacit obedience to immoral laws. By withholding our cooperation, boycotting registration, and standing in solidarity with thousands of other resisters, the Selective Service System law will be made inoperative and unenforceable.

National Resistance Committee
Spring 1980

Compulsory military registration and service prior to congressional approval of war are unwarranted, dangerous and possibly illegal...

Equally as troubling is the extent to which the draft facilitates involvement in foreign conflicts. As the Vietnam War again illustrates, the burden of stopping an undeclared war through congressional action is exceptionally difficult, no matter how wrong the war, and the burden is rightfully and constitutionally placed on the President to demonstrate to Congress the need for a draft at time of war...

We are equally as opposed to a system of universal registration for military service in the future as we are to the actual draft. The registration system facilitates actual conscription, and we believe that it is being offered as a first step in that direction...

Congressional Black Caucus
June 1979

Sisterhood is international—it does not stop at international borders. If we embrace militarism and conscription as part of equality we will be declaring our sisters as enemies. That is something we as women and as feminists *will never* do. We must refuse the mad rush toward military confrontation. Sisterhood is powerful. Say NO to registration; say NO to the draft.

Women's International League for Peace and Freedom
January 1980

I can well understand that you, a young man full of life, loving and loved by your mother, friends, perhaps a young woman, think with a natural terror about what awaits you if you refuse conscription; and perhaps you will not feel strong enough to bear the consequences of refusal, and knowing your weakness, will submit and become a soldier. I understand completely, and I do not for a moment allow myself to blame you, knowing very well that in your place I might perhaps do the same thing. Only do not say that you did it because it was useful or because everyone does it. If you did it, know that you did wrong.

Leo Tolstoy

The first responsibility of a person conscientiously opposed to a particular institution is to refuse to cooperate with—or be a part of—that institution....What I am advocating is draft *resistance*, not draft *evasion*. People who oppose the draft because of deeply held moral or religious reasons—because they believe that war is a crime against humanity—should *publicly* refuse to register.

Refusing to register is the most *effective* way to manifest opposition to the current nature and direction of American foreign policy. I advocate this even though I realize that in so doing I may be violating the Selective Service law.

Jerry Elmer
Field Secretary, Rhode Island
American Friends Service Committee

If Congress votes for registration, War Resisters League supports all those who refuse to register. If one person refuses, the State will jail that person as an example. If a hundred refuse, the State will arrest them as a warning. If a thousand refuse to register, the State will arrest them as a threat to public order. But if a hundred thousand openly refuse to register, the President cannot enforce the law and no arrests will occur.

War Resisters League
Spring 1980

The issue is not equal treatment under compulsion, but freedom from compulsion.

American Friends Service Committee

I hold sacred all life and try to live in that spirit which removes all suffering. Because of my beliefs I must in all conscience work to defeat registration, the draft and the militarization of all society.

Glenda Poole
peace and social activist
mother of two sons

If these efforts should prove fruitless and our government reinstitutes draft registration, I shall, with the assistance of God, encourage, aid and abet all young persons to become nonregistrants. I shall advise these same young people on the evils of compliance with a system of militarization designed to maim and kill other people because of disputes which our leaders are either incapable of or unwilling to solve.

Glenda Poole
peace and social activist

They will tell you to register and be a man. Don't confuse manhood with machoism. A man is a mature person. A mature person recognizes the need for creative, not destructive acts. Your father and I have tried to teach you that no person is your enemy. Hunger, disease, servitude, fear of the unknown are enemies. They are the things a man should want to conquer, not people or nations....War is destructive...to destroy is not manly.

Madge Micheels-Cyrus
A Mother's Letter to Her Son...on Reaching Draft Age

Your father and I have tried to teach you that violence brings violence. It is courageous to love, to care for life, because it means a constant vigilance against any person or any government which dishonors life. War dishonors life.

Madge Micheels-Cyrus
A Mother's Letter to Her Son...on Reaching Draft Age

There are people across the United States who say "YES" to those who say "NO."

Anonymous

(See also Chapter 1—**Militarism**—page 10.)

ADDITIONS:

ADDITIONS:

25
Challenge to Make Peace

A. Facing the Nuclear Reality
B. Silence and Conformity
C. Challenge to the Individual
D. Challenge to the Collective Conscience
E. Challenge to the Nation

A. Facing the Nuclear Reality

* If atomic bombs are to be added as new weapons to the arsenals of a warring world, or to the arsenals of nations preparing for war, then the time will come when mankind will curse the names of Los Alamos and Hiroshima.

J. Robert Oppenheimer
headed the Manhattan Project
which built the atom bomb

What the world is dealing with, then, is not a problem of machines, but of the mind. And the mind has had a very odd relationship with the bomb from the moment it conceived it....The mind made the bomb, the mind denied it, and the mind can stop it cold. If that should sound impossible, consider how impossible nuclear fission must have seemed at the start, or how impossible the Holocaust, or how impossible to the children of Hiroshima that August 6, 1945, would turn out to be anything but another summer day.

It is time to see the bomb as a real weapon again, and not as an amorphous threat or a political lever. It is time to look straight at its drab snout and recall quite clearly what it once did and still can do.

Roger Rosenblatt
Time
July 1981

We've become immersed in dehumanized technicalities and statistics and as a result we have lost the elementary fundamental sense of horror and anguish that is needed to make us see the truth...we can reach back—and we should—through the years to the bombing of Hiroshima and Nagasaki and recover many things we would rather forget.

John Culver
former Senator, Iowa

Here I was, a young physician with good medical training behind me, a chest of all the best medicines then known to science, and I was powerless to help these atomic bomb victims in any way. This was true horror...

I do not want physicians ever again to have to face a landscape of six inches of black ashes, twisted metal beams, severe leukemia, and sizzled bone marrow—and know that they can do nothing.

Nuclear war has been called unthinkable, but our governments continue to prepare for it. To me, what is unthinkable is not to speak out.

Charles S. Stevenson
first American physician in
Nagasaki after the atomic bombing
Physicians for Social Responsibility

Some of what I...describe is horrifying. I know, because it horrifies me. There is a tendency—psychiatrists call it "denial"—to put it out of our minds, not to think about it. But if we are to deal intelligently, wisely, with the nuclear arms race, then we must steel ourselves to contemplate the horrors of nuclear war.

Carl Sagan
The Nuclear Winter

After a nuclear exchange not even the most ardent ideologue is going to be able to tell the ashes of communism from the ashes of free enterprise.

John Kenneth Galbraith

Since nuclear armaments here and in the Soviet Union have created a world in which the whole can nowhere be protected against its parts, our own national security has reached the zero point. The issue is no longer the survival of one nation against another. We stand now in mortal danger of global human incineration.

Episcopal House of Bishops
Pastoral Letter
1980

No one wants to kill another family's child, or another child's family. Yet we prepare to do so.

Karol Schulkin

The last major childhood disease remains and it's the worst of them all: nuclear war.

Beverly Sills
opera star

Human rights, civil rights, women's rights are meaningless before the greatest issue of all—nuclear war and our survival.
Brigadier-General B. K. Gorwitz

Women's rights, men's rights—human rights—all are threatened by the ever-present spectre of war so destructive now of human material and moral values as to render victory indistinguishable from defeat.

Rosika Schwimmer

Nuclear weapons threaten the most basic of human rights—the right to life. **Anonymous**

Nuclear war. It's deadly. And it could affect more children than have ever suffered in the whole history of the world. Two hundred million. Eight hundred million. Nobody knows.... This is the only issue I've ever worked for. I believe, right now, it is the only issue.

Sally Field, actress

Superintendents and curriculum specialists place "nuclear disarmament" on a par with "pollution of the earth's environment" as the social issue most significant for humankind.

Stanley M. Elam
"Educators and the Nuclear Threat"
Phi Delta Kappan

I share your sense that all other current issues pale into footnotes to history in comparison with issues of nuclear war.

Nannerl O. Koehone
President, Wellesley College

This is not an issue. This is survival! It should not be political or partisan. Nor for Democrats or Republicans. It's survival. Period. Both countries have gone past any sensible assessment of the problem...if this problem is not solved soon I really have little faith that the world can continue.

Joanne Woodward
actress

There is no issue more important than the avoidance of nuclear war. Whatever your interests, passions or goals, they and you are threatened fundamentally by the prospect of nuclear war. We have achieved the capability for the certain destruction of our civilization and perhaps of our species as well. I find it incredible that any thinking person would not be concerned in the deepest way about this issue.

...The Earth is an anomaly; in all the Solar System it is, so far as we know, the only inhabited planet. I look at the fossil record and I see that after flourishing for 180 million years the dinosaurs were extinguished. Every last one. There are none left. No species is guaranteed its tenure on this planet. And we've been here for only about a million years, we, the first species that has devised the means for its self-destruction. We are rare and precious because we are alive, because we can think. We are privileged to live, to influence and control our future. I believe we have an obligation to fight for that life, to struggle not just for ourselves, but for all those creatures who came before us, and to whom we are beholden, and for all those who, if we are wise enough, will come after us. There is no cause more urgent, no dedication more fitting for us, than to strive to eliminate the threat of nuclear war. No social convention, no political system, no economic hypothesis, no religious dogma is more important.

Carl Sagan
To Preserve a World Graced by Life

We are all in a great big huge emergency room and we have no doctors to heal us but ourselves.

Barbara Bialick
A Planetary Healing Crisis

We are going to have to find a way to immunize people against the kind of thinking that leads to self-devastation. In effect, we are the malignant virus that is capable of self-destruction.

Jonas Salk

This is the only time in history where humans have the capacity to destroy the world completely. And it could be done by mistake.

Eloy Alfaro
assistant rector, University of Peace

* Mankind faces extinction either through a nuclear or an environmental catastrophe unless humanity changes its ways.

19 Nobel Prize winners and leaders
of about 100 of the country's
environmental and arms control groups

In fact, I think we are in a really close race between our ability to change and our capacity to self-destruct.

Rusty Schweickart
Apollo astronaut

We are reaching a point where more armaments are making the world less safe from a nuclear holocaust. This could be our last chance to say no to the next batch of weaponry.

Owen Chamberlain
Nobel Laureate

Before it is too late, we must narrow the gaping chasm between our proclamations of peace and our lowly deeds which precipitate and perpetuate war. We are called upon to look up from the quagmire of military programs and defense commitments and read the warnings on history's signposts.

One day we must come to see that peace is not merely a distant goal that we seek but a means by which we arrive at that goal. We must pursue peaceful ends through peaceful means. How much longer must we play at deadly war games before we heed the plaintive pleas of the unnumbered dead and maimed of past wars?

Martin Luther King, Jr.

The insistent awareness of absurdity gives us the incentive for radical new approaches and at the same time energizes even the more limited methodical efforts. It is when we lose our sense of nuclear absurdity that we surrender to the forces of annihilation and cease to imagine the real.

Robert Jay Lifton and Richard Falk
Indefensible Weapons

* Unconditional war can no longer lead to unconditional victory. It can no longer serve to settle disputes. It can no longer be of concern to great powers alone. For a nuclear disaster, spread by the winds and waters of fear, could well engulf the great and the small, the rich and the poor, the committed and the uncommitted alike. Mankind must put an end to war or war will put an end to mankind.

John F. Kennedy

* Almost imperceptibly, over the last four decades, every nation and every human being has lost ultimate control over their life and death. For all of us, it is a small group of men and machines in cities far away who can decide our fate. Every day we remain alive is a day of grace, as if mankind as a whole were a prisoner in the death cell awaiting the uncertain moment of execution....A halt to the nuclear arms race is at the present moment imperative.

The Delhi Declaration
signed by the heads of state of Argentina,
Greece, India, Mexico, Sweden and Tanzania

We are confronted here, my friends, with two courses. At the end of the one lies hope—faint hope, if you will—uncertain hope, hope surrounded with dangers, if you insist. At the end of the other lies, so far as I am able to see, no hope at all.

George Kennan
former US Ambassador to the USSR

Behind the black portent of the new atomic age lies a hope which, seized upon with faith, can work out salvation....Let us not deceive ourselves; we must elect world peace or world destruction.

Bernard Baruch
speech to the UN Atomic Energy Commission
August 1946

Science has made unrestricted national sovereignty incompatible with human survival. The only possibilities are now world government or death.

Bertrand Russell

* Through the release of atomic energy, our generation brought into the world the most revolutionary force since prehistoric man's discovery of fire. This basic power of the universe cannot be fitted into the outmoded concept of narrow nationalisms. For there is no secret and there is no defense, there is no possibility of control except through the aroused understanding and insistence of the peoples of the world.

Albert Einstein

Only when American citizens understand that the threat of nuclear war is not something "over there"—in Europe, in the Soviet Union, or in some remote desert factory, but right here at home, no farther away than the next truck on the freeway, might they take the action necessary to end the arms race.

Samuel H. Day, Jr.
The Progressive, **November 1984**

The growing controversy surrounding nuclear fission is the most important issue the American society and the world has ever faced. A national and international debate on this subject is long overdue, and the participation of each individual will determine its outcome. We must begin today by first of all learning as much as we can about the critical issues involved, because what we don't know may kill us. We need new creative initiatives to avoid nuclear catastrophe, and they must begin with awareness, concern and action on the part of the individual.

Dr. Helen Caldicott
founder and past president
Physicians for Social Responsibility

American political and military leaders should publicly acknowledge that there is no realistic prospect for a successful population defense, certainly for many decades, and probably never.

Harold Brown
former Secretary of Defense

Being an ingenious people, Americans find it hard to believe there is no forseeable defense against atomic bombs. But this is a basic fact. Scientists do not even know of any field which promises us any hope of adequate defense.

Albert Einstein

There is no civil defense against nuclear war except prevention of nuclear war.

Paul Warnke
SALT II negotiator

The nuclear bomb is an equal opportunity destroyer.

Ron Dellums
Congressperson, California

The Story of The Bomb: No place to hide.

Randy L.
Boston
Age 8
Please Save My World

...just as the sun shines on the godly and the ungodly alike, so does nuclear radiation. And with this knowledge it becomes increasingly difficult to embrace the thought of extinction purely for the assumed satisfaction of—from the grave—achieving revenge. Or even of accepting our demise as a planet as a simple and just preventive medicine administered to the universe. Life is better than death, I believe, if only because it is less boring, and because it has fresh peaches in it.

Alice Walker
author

Everybody knows there will always be wars, right? Wrong! Everybody knows there will always be *conflict*. For a growing number of nations possessing nuclear weapons, attempting to settle conflict with war isn't an option anymore.

Jeanne Larson

When we get to the point, as we one day will, that both sides know that in any outbreak of general hostilities, regardless of the element of surprise, destruction will be both reciprocal and complete, possibly we will have sense enough to meet at the conference table with the understanding that the era of armaments has ended and the human race must conform its actions to this truth or die.

Dwight D. Eisenhower
April 1956

* We must remold the relationships of all men, of all nations in such a way that these men do not wish, or dare, to fall upon each other for the sake of vulgar, outdated ambition or for passionate differences in ideologies, and that international bodies by supreme authority may give peace on earth and justice among men.

Winston Churchill
House of Commons
August 1945

But this very triumph of scientific annihilation—this very success of invention—has destroyed the possibility of war's being a medium for the practical settlement of international differences. The enormous destruction to both sides of closely matched opponents makes it impossible for even the winner to translate it into anything but his own disaster.

General Douglas MacArthur
July 1961

There is no political reason on earth that can morally justify the continued uncontrolled existence of these weapons.   **Christine Cassel**
Physicians for Social Responsibility

There is nothing, except a tragic death wish, to prevent us from re-ordering our priorities, so that the pursuit of peace will take precedence over the pursuit of war.

Martin Luther King, Jr.

We recognize that once a civilization has invented nuclear weapons, the only alternative to self-destruction is to invent peace. War has been made obsolete.

Women's Peace Presence

All war must be declared obsolete in the nuclear age.   **Irene Brown**

Peace is the one condition of survival in this nuclear age.

Adlai E. Stevenson

The way to win an atomic war is to make certain it never starts.

General Omar Bradley

The hydrogen bomb is history's exclamation point. It ends an age-long sentence of manifest violence.

Marshall McLuhan

I think both the Soviets and the U.S. are very dangerous governments building up very dangerous weapons. I don't care who is ahead, because if there is a nuclear war we'll all be wiped out. We're past the point of it making any sense who is ahead.

Zafra Epstein
Age 13
Our Future at Stake

The arms race is just silly to me, and it's gone on for so long. One government thinks "If I stop now, the other countries will hurt me," but the building up just increases all of our chances of mistakes or someone using them. Communication and understanding would work much better than threats, and it could not be more expensive or take more effort than the arms race does, could it? We should all at least just stop now for a breather and think for a while. Even just a one-year breather in the arms race would give us a chance to be more rational about it.

Wenonah Elms
Age 13
Our Future at Stake

I have this image of what this missile stuff is all about and that is that somehow these nations were big boys or brothers fighting in the alley and waiting for a parent to come out and break them up....It started dawning on me that there weren't any parents to break them up—all there was was just kids,...the whole world was just kids.

Paul Paulos

We must raise the question with utmost urgency: are nuclear arsenals poised to destroy entire civilizations realistic methods of keeping us from harm?

Fellowship of Reconciliation

[Referring to nuclear weapons and the direct disarmament movement]
They're going to get us or we're going to get them.
Philip Berrigan

We will have "Star Wars" or arms control. We can't have both.
Clark Clifford
former Secretary of Defense

As few as 100 nuclear weapons on each side, half of one per cent of the
current arsenals, could devastate the US and the USSR beyond any
historical experience and perhaps beyond recovery as industrial societies.
To end the danger of nuclear war the nations must not merely freeze
nuclear weapons but abolish them.
Randall Forsberg
Scientific American, **November 1982**

The end of further experiments with atom bombs would be like the early
sunrays of hope which suffering humanity is longing for.
Albert Schweitzer

For while unilateral disarmament poses a *risk*, the paranoid-technocratic
confrontation between superpowers poses a *certainty*: extermination
through nuclear holocaust.
Joel Kovel

We balance the risks of an unarmed world against one with nuclear
weapons and we know that while capitalism and communism as they
now exist would not survive disarmament, humanity would.
David McReynolds

Many more nations have been brought to destruction by fear of change
than by love of it.
Bertrand Russell

Death can never be overcome without danger.   **Greek wisdom**

If the human race wishes to have a prolonged and indefinite period of
material prosperity, they have only got to behave in a peaceful and helpful
way toward one another.   **Winston Churchill**

* We, the citizens of Hiroshima, ever mindful of this cruel experience,
clearly foresee the extinction of mankind and an end to civilization should
the world drift into a nuclear war. Therefore, we have vowed to set aside
our griefs and grudges and continuously plead before the peoples of the
world to abolish weapons and renounce war so that we may never again
repeat the tragedy of Hiroshima.   **Takeshi Araki**
Mayor of Hiroshima
August 1976

B. Silence and Conformity

Time changes; truth is altered. We must perceive and react from what we understand at this moment in time.

Henry Ibsen

At present, most of us do nothing. We look away. We remain calm. We are silent.

Jonathan Schell
The Fate of the Earth

Most of us build prisons for ourselves, and after we occupy them for a period of time we become accustomed to their walls and accept the false premise that we are incarcerated for life. As soon as that belief takes hold of us we abandon hope of ever doing more with our lives and of ever giving our dreams a chance to be fulfilled. We begin to suffer living deaths; one of a herd heading for destruction in a grey mass of mediocrity.

Barb Katt
on being sentenced for destroying
a war-related computer at Sperry Corp.

Why weren't there Germans blockading the tracks to Auschwitz?

Daniel Ellsberg

I have often wondered what I would have done if I were a German in the '40s watching the boxcars of people pass through my town. Would I have left it to someone else to step forward, to raise the question, to try to stop the trains?

Karol Schulkin
reflecting on nuclear weapons
the equivalent of nuclear ovens
Ground Zero, **Spring 1983**

In Germany they first came for the Communists and I didn't speak up because I wasn't a Communist. Then they came for the Jews, and I didn't speak up because I wasn't a Jew. Then they came for the trade unionists, and I didn't speak up because I wasn't a trade unionist. Then they came for the Catholics, and I didn't speak up because I was a Protestant. Then they came for me—and by that time no one was left to speak up.

Pastor Martin Niemöller

"Good Germans" is the phrase historians use to describe a people who silently go along with their government's grand plans for military adventures. If the madness of World War III really is upon us, perhaps this is the era of Good Americans.   **Colman McCarthy**
1980

The violence is here; it is a fact. Injustice exists; this is reality. As Christians we may not abide this. We may not allow ourselves to grow accustomed to evil, least of all to an evil that is daily and constant. We may not keep silent, especially when people try to intimidate us with threats, campaigns of vilification, and reprisals.

**Declaration of the International
Meeting of Latin American Bishops
November/December 1977**

It may well be that the greatest tragedy of this period of social transition is not the glaring noisiness of the so-called bad people, but the appalling silence of the so-called good people.

Martin Luther King, Jr.

The sin of omission—the refusal to get involved—is one of the worst things in the world.

**Adolfo Pérez Esquivel
1980 Nobel Peace Prize
*Christ in a Poncho***

The hottest places in hell are reserved for those who, in time of great moral crisis, maintain their neutrality.

Dante

We know what happens to people who stay in the middle of the road. They get run over.

Aneurin Bevan

Nothing will ever be attempted if all possible objections must be first overcome.

Samuel Johnson

All we need for the triumph of evil is that good people do nothing.

Edmund Burke

* I have thought for a long time now that if, someday, the increasing efficiency of the technique of destruction finally causes our species to disappear from the earth, it will not be cruelty that will be responsible for our extinction and still less, of course, the indignation that cruelty awakens and the reprisals and vengeance that it brings upon itself...but the docility, the lack of responsibility of the modern man, his base subservient acceptance of every common decree. The horrors which we have seen, the still greater horrors we shall presently see, are not signs that rebels, insubordinate, untameable men, are increasing in number throughout the world, but rather that there is a constant increase, a stupendously rapid increase, in the number of obedient, docile men.

**Georges Bernanos
French writer**

We will never understand totalitarianism if we do not understand that people rarely have the strength to be uncommon...

Eugène Ionesco

[Children should be taught] to resist unjust or ridiculous authority....The worst thing...is how easily people can be led by any kind of authority figure, or even the most minimal signs of authority....We put up a sign on the road "Delaware closed today." Motorists didn't question it. Instead they asked,"Is Jersey open?"

Allen Funt
Candid Camera
May 1985

The evils of government are directly proportional to the tolerance of the people.

Frank Kent

The limits of tyrants are prescribed by the endurance of those whom they oppress.

Frederick Douglass

There is no slavery where there are no willing slaves.

Jose Riza
Filipino patriot

The essence of power is not in military might but in the people. They are ruled by the state to the degree that they cooperate with the state. The state loses its power to the degree that the people withdraw or sever their cooperation.

Gene Sharp

* The land of propaganda is built on unanimity. If one man says "NO," the spell is broken and public order is endangered.

Ignazio Silone
Bread and Wine

There must have been a time, near the beginning, when we could have said "No."

Tom Stoppard
Rosencrantz and Guildenstern Are Dead
(A play taking off from the plot of *Hamlet*)

They that give up essential liberty to obtain a little temporary safety deserve neither liberty nor safety.

Benjamin Franklin

* To sin by silence when they should protest makes cowards of men.

Abraham Lincoln

Cowards die many times before their deaths, the valiant never taste of death but once.

William Shakespeare
Julius Caesar

Something we were withholding made us weak. Until we found it was ourselves.

Robert Frost

Far more violence to human beings in history has been done in obeying the law than in breaking the law.

Howard Zenn
Lovejoy's Nuclear War

Conforming has killed more people—though perhaps more slowly—than rebelling; and especially the millions, in all countries, who conventionally tramped off to wars that accomplished nothing except keeping the map-makers busy.

Anonymous

A common and natural result of an undue respect for law is, that you may see a file of soldiers, colonel, captain, corporal, privates, powder-monkeys, and all, marching in admirable order over hill and dale to the wars, against their wills, ay, against their common sense and consciences, which makes it very steep marching indeed, and produces a palpitation of the heart. They have no doubt that it is a damnable business in which they are concerned; they are all peaceably inclined...

Henry David Thoreau

When great changes occur in history, when great principles are involved, as a rule the majority are wrong.

Eugene Debs

A very great historic change that has been based upon nonconformity, has been bought either with the blood or with the reputation of nonconformists.

Ben Shahn

The moment we begin to fear the opinions of others and hesitate to tell the truth that is in us, and from motives of policy are silent when we should speak, the divine floods of light and life flow no longer into our souls....Every truth we see is ours to give the world, not to keep to ourselves alone, for in doing so we cheat humanity out of their rights and check our own development.

Elizabeth Cady Stanton

* The reasonable man adapts himself to the world; the unreasonable one persists in trying to adapt the world to himself. Therefore, all progress depends on the unreasonable man.

George Bernard Shaw

Liberation is an awakening of the consciousness, a change of mentality for ways of thinking so that the person no longer thinks what their present society wants him/her to think but rather learns to think and act for him/herself in dialogue with others in order to create a new world in which it is easier to love.

Magaly Rodriguez O'Hearn

C. Challenge to the Individual

* We have seen the enemy, and he is us.

Walt Kelly
Pogo

Knowing is terrifying
Not knowing is terrifying
But not knowing is hopeless
And knowing may save us.

high school student
Brookline, Massachusetts

On Hiroshima/Nagasaki: To know and not to act is not yet to know.

Anonymous

Extinction is not something to contemplate; it is something to rebel against.

Jonathan Schell
The Fate of the Earth

I will act as if what I do makes a difference.

William James

For it isn't enough to talk about peace. One must believe in it. And it isn't enough to believe in it. One must work at it.

Eleanor Roosevelt

We can begin anywhere—everywhere. "Let there be peace" says a bumper sticker, "and let it begin with me"....Let there be transformation, and let it begin with me.

Marilyn Ferguson

Peace if it is to be mine and shared with the world must begin in me; a personal peace.

Alex Birkholz
7th Grader

It is not yours to finish the task, but neither are you free to take no part in it.
from the Jewish *Wisdom of the Fathers*

Everything now, we must assume, is in our hands; we have no right to assume otherwise.
James Baldwin

It is time for us to raise our voices. No one of us can do everything—but each of us can do something. We can demand a government that embraces life.
Terry Herndon
teacher

Each of us is an expert with the full passion and resources to change the world. We should activate ourselves and not wait for the male experts, but follow the love and the passion in our hearts and our minds to bring about the kind of transformation so our children can live.
Patricia Ellsberg

We should say to each of them: Do you know what you are? You are a marvel. You are unique. In all the world there is no other child exactly like you. In the millions of years that have passed, there has never been a child like you...and when you grow up, can you then harm another who is, like you, a marvel? You must cherish one another. You must work—we must all work—to make this world worthy of its children.
Pablo Casals

There are no sidelines in life. We must enter in and live.
Swami Satchedananda

When somebody says, "Well, there's nothing I can do," I know they're not awake. When you're awake you could use a hundred other people to help you.
Anonymous

No one has a right to sit down and feel hopeless. There's too much work to do.
Dorothy Day

* He who stands for nothing will fall for anything.   **Anonymous**

* If a man doesn't find something to die for he probably hasn't anything to live for.
James Bevel

One has to speak out and stand up for one's convictions. Inaction at a time of conflagration is inexcusable.
Mahatma Gandhi

The ultimate measure of a person is not where they stand in moments of comfort and convenience, but where they stand at times of challenge and controversy.

Martin Luther King, Jr.

Moderation in temper is always a virtue, but moderation in principle is always a vice.

Thomas Paine

It isn't just a question of gender and gaps, of motherhood and morality. It isn't a question of men versus women, but of citizens who do and don't participate. At the core, the arms debate isn't a matter of statistics but of values and choices and that's a language anybody can learn.

Ellen Goodman
columnist

Every person is the right person to act. Every moment is the right moment to begin.

Jonathan Schell
The Fate of the Earth

I am only one, but still I am one. I cannot do everything, but still I can do something; and because I cannot do everything I will not refuse to do the something that I can do.

Edward Everett Hale

I wondered why somebody didn't do something for peace....Then I realized that I am somebody.

Anonymous

Kids know, better than grownups, what we do is more important than what we say.

Pete Seeger

Each one of us has inside a piece of peace that must emerge and live outside us.

Anonymous

It is in each of us that the peace of the world is cast...from there it must spread out to the limits of the universe.

Leo Cardinal Suenens

What I want to bring out is how a pebble cast into a pond causes ripples that spread in all directions. And each one of our thoughts, words and deeds is like that.

Dorothy Day

Putting our money where our hearts are is one more, potentially very powerful way to integrate our lives and work for peace—and a sustainable future.

Susan Meeker-Lowry
co-editor, *Good Money: A Newsletter of Social Investing*

Against the ruin of the world, there is only one defense—the creative act.

Kenneth Rexroth

...You must be a practicing idealist if you are to remain a true idealist for long. You must take small practical steps, often when you would prefer to take giant ones—but you must move in the direction of your ideals through action. Otherwise you will feel disillusioned, or powerless, or sure, again, that only drastic, highly unideal methods will ever bring about the achievement of a given ideal state or situation.

(Seth) Jane Roberts
The Individual and the Nature of Mass Events

The journey of a thousand miles begins with one step.

Lao-tse

The journey of a thousand leagues begins with a single step. So we must never neglect any work of peace within our reach, however small.

Adlai E. Stevenson

Every citizen who loves this country, its freedom and good life; every parent whose children yearn for their day in the sun; every American who believes our national heritage still represents "the last, best hope of earth," must become earnestly engaged in the active quest for peace.

Frank Church
former Senator, Idaho

Ask not what your country can do for you, but rather what you can do for your country.

John F. Kennedy
quoting Seneca

In light of my faith, I am prepared to live without nuclear weapons in my country.

Fellowship of Reconciliation

I have an 8-month-old daughter and I'm very concerned about a nuclear war. I look at my baby girl and wonder what, if any, kind of future she will have. I feel that everyone has a responsibility to do what they can...I couldn't live with myself if I didn't try to do something. I love my daughter too much.

Debra J. Elslager

I don't want my children coming up to me and saying, now what did you do, and me saying I didn't know.

Dorothee Sölle

* Every thoughtful citizen who despairs of war and wishes to bring peace should begin by looking inward, by examining his own attitudes toward the possibilities of peace, toward the Soviet Union, toward the course of the cold war, and toward freedom and peace here at home.

John F. Kennedy

* Let us examine our attitude toward peace itself. Too many of us think it is impossible. Too many think it unreal. But that is a dangerous, defeatist belief. It leads to the conclusion that war is inevitable, that mankind is doomed, that we are gripped by forces we cannot control.

John F. Kennedy

* Our problems are man made. Therefore, they can be solved by man. And man can be as big as he wants. No problem of human destiny is beyond human beings. Man's reason and spirit have often solved the seemingly unsolvable, and we believe they can do it again.

John F. Kennedy

* Samantha couldn't accept man's inhumanity to man. She stood fast in the belief that peace can be achieved and maintained by mankind.

Samantha Smith
13-year-old peace activist
as described by her mother
after Samantha's death in a plane crash
1985

* For without belittling the courage with which men have died, we should not forget those acts of courage with which men...have lived....A man does that which he must—in spite of personal consequences, in spite of obstacles and dangers and pressures—and that is the basis of all human morality.

John F. Kennedy

Each time a person stands for an ideal, or acts to improve the lot of others, or strikes out against injustice, he or she sends forth a tiny ripple of hope. And crossing each other from a million different centers of energy and daring, those ripples build a current that can sweep down the mightiest walls of oppression and resistance. Few are willing to brave the disapproval of their fellows, the censure of their colleagues, the wrath of their society. Moral courage is a rarer commodity than bravery in battle or great intelligence. Yet it is the one essential vital quality for those who seek to change a world that yields most painfully to change.

Robert F. Kennedy

We may be frightened of taking risks, not knowing what will happen to us, of standing out by making a personal statement, of being embarrassed in public...of losing security...or the respect of people we had thought were friends.

Greenham Women Everywhere

Every public reform was once a private opinion.

Ralph Waldo Emerson

It is no dishonor to be in a minority in the cause of liberty and virtue.

Sam Adams
1771

The probability that we may fail in the struggle ought not to deter us from the support of a cause we believe to be just.

Abraham Lincoln

* The men who try to do something and fail are infinitely better than those who try nothing and succeed.

Lloyd Jones

People do not lack strength, they lack will.

Victor Hugo

I realize suddenly that it is not a question of faith, but of will. I *will* life to go on.

We have collectively created the death cults. We can collectively create a culture of life.

But to do so, we must be willing to step out of line, to forgo the comfort of leaving decisions up to somebody else. To will is to make our own decisions, guide our own lives, commit ourselves, our time, our work, our energy, to act in the service of life. To will is to reclaim our power, our power to reclaim the future.

Starhawk
The Spiral Dance

I've been to demonstrations, and the big surprise was that they were fun. Being there with so many people who are there for a sense of purpose makes you feel energy and power.

Caedmon Fujimoto
Age 16
Our Future at Stake

* I have been to demonstrations before and they were fun. I try to think about it like an adventure and then it's not scary. The one thing that really scares me, though, about civil disobedience is what about if I get arrested by a racist police officer and he decides to take it out on me...I want to try it though...I need to try all kinds of ways to protest the arms race, but I'm a little scared.

Ursell Austin
Age 16
Our Future at Stake

I feel that getting involved and trying to do something about nuclear bombs has made me feel much better—a lot less depressed. I'm glad I'm one more person trying to do something about it. It seems to me like this age, 15 years old, is when you really start thinking about things, thinking about your life, and it's good to feel you can do something about the things you don't agree with.

Regina Hunter
Age 15
Our Future at Stake

I think any action is worth doing. Demonstrations make me feel happy and exhilarated. People focus on love of life rather than death or fear. It's great.

Max Friedman
Age 16
Our Future at Stake

I don't think there is any single most effective way to stop this craziness. Everyone has their own way. When people learn about the arms race and get active, each one finds something to do that feels right to them— wearing buttons, praying, writing letters, getting arrested, demonstrating. It all adds up, every little thing we do touches someone. Putting your body on the line may be more dramatic or get more attention from the media, but it's not necessarily more effective than some smaller or quiet things that touch people. Whatever people do is good. But everyone has to do something.

Zafra Epstein
Age 13
Our Future at Stake

As you come to know the seriousness of our situation—the war, the racism, the poverty in the world—you come to realize it is not going to be changed just by words or demonstrations. It's a question of risking your life. It's a question of living your life in drastically different ways.

Dorothy Day

People say to me "What a sacrifice you've made! How brave you are! How much you gave up!" And it makes me want to laugh because I have given up nothing. Nothing. Nothing except irrelevance.

Jane Fonda
actress

The most powerful antinuclear weapon in the world is YOU!

Nuclear Times
March 1983

Nothing could be worse than the fear that one had given up too soon and left one unexpended effort which might have saved the world.

Jane Addams

They were told "No" a thousand times and after the final "No" there was a "Yes" that saved the world.

Wallace Stevens

D. Challenge to the Collective Conscience

Can one generation bind another and all others in succession forever? I think not. The Creator made the earth for the living not the dead.

Thomas Jefferson
1781

We must never relax our efforts to arouse in the people of the world, and especially in their governments, an awareness of the unprecedented disaster which they are absolutely certain to bring on themselves unless there is a fundamental change in their attitudes toward one another as well as in their concept of the future.

Albert Einstein

* The unleashed power of the atom has changed everything save our modes of thinking, and thus we drift toward unparalleled catastrophe. We shall require a substantially new manner of thinking if mankind is to survive.

Albert Einstein

This generation has, quite humbly, the final responsibility and the last chance to turn terror into hope.   Albert Einstein

Increasingly, it is evident that our generation has arrived at a turning point. Will we indeed fulfill the theory that our species is fatally flawed because it is incapable of controlling its aggressive tendencies and is, therefore, destined for extinction or will we move in a fresh direction toward a disarmed world?   Fellowship of Reconciliation

If you put a frog into a pot of boiling water, the frog will jump out. However, if you put a frog in a pot of cold water and slowly raise the temperature, the frog will boil to death.

When it comes to the military preparations going on around us, do we recognize the rise in temperature?

Rosalie Bertell
biostatistician

The overwhelming priority to do away with nuclear arms has not penetrated the collective consciousness or conscience of the general public....Nuclear arms must not just be limited, they must be eliminated.

Reverend Maurice McCrackin
Community Church of Cincinnati

Probably every generation sees itself as charged with remaking the world. Mine, however, knows it will not remake the world. Its task is even greater: to keep the world from destroying itself.

Albert Camus

We who are about to die demand a miracle.

W. H. Auden

* Shall we put an end to the human race or shall man renounce war?

Albert Einstein

We still have a choice today: non-violent co-existence or violent co-annihilation. We must move past indecision to action. Now let us begin. Now let us rededicate ourselves to the long and bitter—but beautiful—struggle for a new world...The choice is ours, and though we might prefer it otherwise, we must choose in this crucial moment of human history.

Martin Luther King, Jr.

* Removing the threat of a world war—a nuclear war—is the most acute and urgent task of the present day. Mankind is confronted with a choice: we must halt the arms race and proceed to disarmament or face annihilation.

Final Document
U.N. Special Session on Disarmament
1978

For with the advent of atomic weapons we have come either to the last page of war, at any rate on the major international scale we have known in the past, or to the last page of history.

B. H. Liddell Hart
Why Don't We Learn from History?

* We must learn to live together as brothers or we are going to perish together as fools.

Martin Luther King, Jr.

We can look at it now in one of two ways. This is the end and we might as well get over it...or this is the hard birth of the new age.

Ram Dass

If we let it, the Bomb can provide us with the necessary stress...to create the unity which [could bring forth] the new age.

Joanna Rogers Macy

For, although it is true that fear and despair can overwhelm us, hope cannot be purchased with the refusal to feel.

Susan Griffin

Nuclear war is inevitable, says the pessimist;
Nuclear war is impossible, says the optimist;
Nuclear war is inevitable unless we make it impossible, says the realist.

Sydney J. Harris
columnist

* These are the times for real choices and not false ones. We are at the moment when our lives must be placed on the line if our nation is to survive its own folly. Everyone of humane convictions must decide on the protest that best suits his convictions, but we all must protest.

Martin Luther King, Jr.

For the love of God, your children and the civilization to which you belong, cease the madness. You have a duty not just to the generation of the present: you have a duty to civilizations past, which you threaten to render meaningless, and to its future, which you threaten to render nonexistent.

George Kennan
former US Ambassador to the USSR

We are faced with the fact that tomorrow is today. We are confronted with the fierce urgency of now. In this unfolding conundrum of life and history there is such a thing as being too late. Procrastination is still the thief of time.

Martin Luther King, Jr.

If we are to survive on this planet, the arms race must be slowed, stopped, and reversed. The time to start is now.

Rear Admiral Gene R. La Rocque
US Navy (retired)

There is no time left for anything but to make peace work a dimension of our every waking activity.

Elise Boulding

* ...Today we have achieved—we and the Russians together—in the creation of these devices and their means of delivery, levels of redundancy of such grotesque dimensions as to defy rational understanding. What a confession of intellectual poverty it would be, what a bankruptcy of intelligent statesmanship, if we had to admit that such blind, senseless acts of destruction were the best we could do.

George Kennan
former US Ambassador to the USSR

Wars can be prevented just as surely as they can be provoked, and we who fail to prevent them must share in the guilt for the dead.

General Omar Bradley

War is not created by basic human aggressiveness, war is organized! Peace has to be organized even more effectively!

The Great Peace Journey
Swedish brochure
1985

...because we want peace with half a heart and half a life and will, the war, of course, continues because the waging of war, by its nature, is total—but the waging of peace, by our own cowardice, is partial. So a whole will and a whole heart and a whole national life bent toward war prevail over the [mere desire for] peace...

Daniel Berrigan

Events have proved the futility of war, but war still rules the world because its uncompromising opponents are too few.

Jesse Wallace Hughan

There is no peace because there are no peacemakers, there are no peacemakers because the making of peace is at least as costly as the making of war.

Daniel Berrigan

We cannot have peace if we are only concerned with peace. War is not an accident. It is the logical outcome of a certain way of life. If we want to attack war, we have to attack that way of life.

A. J. Muste

Very few people chose war. They chose selfishness and the result was war. Each of us, individually and nationally, must choose: total love or total war.

Dave Dellinger
statement on entering prison
1943

Destructive power inherent in matter must be controlled by the idealism of the spirit and the wisdom of the mind. They alone stand between us and a lifeless planet.

John Foster Dulles

Two thousand years ago a Roman noble said: "If you would have peace, prepare for war." For two thousand years men have been preparing for war—and fighting wars. Women know we are preparing for a war right now. This time a nuclear war in which there will be no winner. We realize that we must begin to prepare for peace if we want a future for our children.

Joanne Woodward
actress

The lessons of Hiroshima and Nagasaki go unnoticed as governments continue to develop nuclear arms and nuclear power....Primarily it is women who are involved in the struggle to sustain and maintain life....Women are speaking and struggling toward rebirth for the life of the planet and the children.

Linda Hagan
Chickasaw Nation

It has been a woman's task throughout history to go on believing in life when there was almost no hope. If we are united, we may be able to produce a world in which our children and other people's children can be safe.

Margaret Mead
anthropologist

* An earth fit for growing children is what every woman should work for.

Lillian Smith

I, too, believe that one of our greatest hopes lies in mobilizing the passion we have as women for the survival of our children.

Patricia Ellsberg

If we want to survive we must love our children more than we hate and fear our enemies.

Irene Brown
Michigan activist

We must have the strength to recall to our fellow Americans that to be loyal to this country does Not, Not, Not compel us to be disloyal to the human species, to all life on the planet.   **Daniel Ellsberg**

Those nuclear weapons are aimed at you and me, our friends, our neighbors, our kids. We have to aim back with our votes, with our petitions, with our voices, to tell the people in Congress, in the White House, in the Pentagon, here and in the Soviet Union, and all over the world, that people want to live.

Bella Abzug
former Congressperson,
New York

We have the obligation to create a world order in which we neither have to kill or be killed.

A Human Manifesto by Planetary Citizens

World peace starts right here. I will not raise my child to kill your child.

Barbara Choo

If we are to reach real peace in this world and if we are to carry on a real war against war, we shall have to begin with the children.

Mahatma Gandhi

If we really acquire this will to peace, we will gradually impart it to our children, but we will have to give them something to take the place of the adventure and excitement of war. We will have to go even further and devise something to take the place of the sacrifice which is so great an element in patriotism and which no matter how selfish youth may be, is the element in their nature which drives them to deeds of heroism and to heights of unselfish devotion which they would be incapable of except in times when they feel the call to be somewhat greater than they really are....This challenge to organize a new social order not in one place, but all over the world, has possibilities of adventure and excitement, a society which of itself should take the place of the old glamour surrounding war. Only women and the youth of any country can initiate this change.

Eleanor Roosevelt

If peace...only had the music and pageantry of war, there'd be no more wars.

Sophie Kerr

I have decided for what remains of my life to be an activist....And I ask you to join all of us out here who want to see—for you and your children—a survival, a solution—to find the dignity of peace.

Stanley Kramer
film maker

The signers of this declaration pledge to commit ourselves to work unceasingly to establish a just peace, to reverse the "arms race" both nuclear and conventional, and to completely dismantle all nuclear weapons, that the children of the world may be free of the threat of nuclear war and may share in a beneficent and bountiful future.

Hiroshima/Nagasaki Committee
Washington, D.C.
1985

Let's be in peace with each other and not in pieces with each other.

Nicholas Lorberter
5th Grader

* Somehow we must transform the dynamics of the world power struggle from the negative nuclear arms race, which no one can win, to a positive contest to harness man's creative genius for the purpose of making peace and prosperity a reality for all nations of the world.

Martin Luther King, Jr.

We need not only a moral equivalent to war, as William James called for, but also a politically effective substitute....Those of us who oppose the violence of the status quo and reject the violence of armed revolt and class hatred bear a heavy responsibility to struggle existentially to provide nonviolent alternatives.

Dave Dellinger
Revolutionary Nonviolence

We have it in our power to begin the world again.

Thomas Paine

Future people will wonder why we endured so many evils which we had the power to change.

Ashleigh Brilliant

The ultimate power is always in people—in their will to resist.

Ralph Templin
Democracy and Nonviolence

This revolution is not being made through military power. It is people power!

Fidel Ramos
Philippine Deputy Armed Forces Chief
February 1986

* The joke told and retold all over was about a meeting of Marcos strategists in Manila. One strategist told Marcos: "Mr. President, we will win. We can't lose at all. The Batasan members are ours, the governors are ours, the mayors are ours, the village heads are ours, the military are ours, the judges are ours, the poll chairmen are ours, the Comelec [Commission on Elections] are ours. How can we lose?" To which one meek soul spoke faintly just above a whisper, "But Mr. President, the people are not ours."

Eliezer D. Mapanao
President, Southern Christian College
Philippines

True the elephant is stronger. But the ants...well, there are more of them.

Adolfo Pérez Esquivel
1980 Nobel Peace Prize
Christ in a Poncho

Histories are *written* by intellectuals, who generally give undue credit to other intellectuals for making history. But history is *made* by people who commit themselves, their lives, and their energies to the struggle.

Dave Dellinger
Revolutionary Nonviolence

We must remember that one determined person can make a significant difference, and that a small group of determined people can change the course of history.

Sonia Johnson

We are malign enough, twisted enough, to bring creation to a smoking ruin;
—we have the instruments.
—we have the myths.
—we even have the blueprints.
They are stashed away in some war room, in some hollowed out mountain. Who will confront this crime?...I think it is only the resisting people. Those who confront weapons, weapons-makers and their immaculate guardian—the law. If a God exists, these are God's people.

Daniel Berrigan
Book of Uncommon Prayer

I know of no safe repository of the ultimate power of society but people. And if we think them not enlightened enough, the remedy is not to take the power from them, but to inform them by education.

Thomas Jefferson
1820

Establishing lasting peace is the work of education; all politics can do is keep us out of war.

Maria Montessori

The facts about nuclear energy must be taken to the village square and from there a decision made about its future.

Albert Einstein

...women all over the country can get to know the facts...so they can stand up and ask the hard questions and say, "We want to be involved in the details of our own protection, rather than trusting it to the same old craziness."

Pat Schroeder
Congressperson, Colorado

By exerting electoral pressure, an aroused citizenry can still move its government to the side of morality and common sense. In fact, the momentum for movement in this direction can only originate in the heart and mind of the individual citizen.

Dr. Helen Caldicott
founder and past president
Physicians for Social Responsibility

No social advance rolls in on the wheels of inevitability. It comes through the tireless efforts and persistent work of dedicated individuals.

Martin Luther King, Jr.

Those who profess to favor freedom and yet depreciate agitation, are people who want crops without ploughing the ground; they want rain without thunder and lightning; they want the ocean without the roar of its many waters. The struggle may be a moral one, or it may be a physical one, or it may be both. But it must be a struggle. Power concedes nothing without a demand; it never has and it never will.

Frederick Douglass
1857

The power of an aroused public is unbeatable. Vietnam and Watergate proved that. It must be demonstrated again. It is not yet too late, for while there is life there is hope. There is no cause for pessimism, for already I have seen great obstacles surmounted. Nor need we be afraid, for I have seen democracy work.

Dr. Helen Caldicott
founder and past president
Physicians for Social Responsibility

While the people retain their virtue and vigilance, no administration, by any extreme of wickedness or folly, can very seriously injure the government in the short space of four years.

Abraham Lincoln

It is a superstition and ungodly thing to believe that an act of a majority binds a minority. Many examples can be given in which acts of majorities will be found to have been wrong and those of minorities to have been right. All reforms owe their origin to the initiation of minorities in opposition to majorities.

Mahatma Gandhi

War is much too serious a matter to be entrusted to the military.

Georges Clemenceau

We need to make sure the decision-makers know that for us there are limits to this absurd stockpiling of nuclear weapons, and for us as believers there is an alternative to mutual nuclear suicide.

John Cardinal Krol
***The Churches and Nuclear War*, September 1979**

We do not have to wait for our political leaders. Mass consciousness regulates behavior far more than the formal laws and controls by which societies attempt to regulate it from the top. This consciousness changes, when it does, by a lot of people changing their minds, sometimes only a little. Such a change in mass consciousness has been the driving force for all the great social transformations in history. Thus, as the word spreads that peace is possible, world consciousness can shift.

Willis W. Harman

There is another major shift in consciousness taking place in the 1980s...the synthesis of personal and planetary concerns—a wedding of psychological, spiritual and political dimensions into a unified approach to change.

Kevin McVeigh
Interhelp

There is a shift at a level below politics which could be more significant than any negotiations taking place in Geneva.

E. P. Thompson

I like to believe that people in the long run are going to do more to promote peace than are governments. Indeed, I think that people want peace so much that one of these days governments had better get out of their way and let them have it.

Dwight D. Eisenhower

* Controlled, universal disarmament is the imperative of our time. The demand for it by the hundreds of millions whose chief concern is the long future of themselves and their children will, I hope, become so universal and so insistent that no man, no government anywhere, can withstand it.

Dwight D. Eisenhower

If we do not change our direction, we are likely to end up where we are headed.

Ancient Chinese proverb

My generation has failed to stop the arms race. But it's really the men who have failed. Now it's up to the women, and I believe they can do it.

Rear Admiral Gene R. La Rocque
U.S. Navy (retired)

Women, if the soul of the nation is to be saved, I believe that you must become its soul.

Coretta Scott King

The will to peace will have to start with women and they will have to want peace sufficiently to be crusaders. It's up to the women.

Eleanor Roosevelt

An aroused woman is unstoppable. We've got the babies.

Dr. Helen Caldicott
founder and past president
Physicians for Social Responsibility

If we are ever going to eliminate the threat of nuclear war, it is going to take the untapped power of American women to help bring it about.

Grace Kennan Warnecke
Business Executives for National Security

What is the arms race and the cold war but the combination of male competitiveness and aggression into the inhuman sphere of computer-run institutions? If women are to cease producing cannon-fodder for the final holocaust, they must rescue men from the perversities of their own polarization.

Germaine Greer
The Female Eunuch

Without new ideas, new leadership and new action by women, men will go on preparing for the next war because they have always prepared for war.

But women know that the next war will be the end of us, our children and our fragile, beautiful planet....

Our only hope is to prevent that war and the decision on how to do that is too important to be left to the men alone.

Joanne Woodward
actress

How will nuclear disarmament conferences be different when the dress code no longer requires suits and ties? Above all, women have the capacity to look afresh at the many problems we face today. Because we have been so totally excluded from decision making in the realm of foreign and national security affairs, we do not have to be defensive about present dead-end policies.

The bright, eager young men—the best and the brightest in David Halberstam's phrase, once so confident as they thought up such things as our triad of strategic forces, by which we divide our nuclear weapons launchers among airplanes, submarines and groundbased systems—these same young men are less cocky, less sure about their creations....A newcomer, who doesn't need to be defensive about past policies because he or she had no part in formulating them, can point out that the triad is not the Holy Trinity.

Dr. Anne H. Cahn

This is a war about which women were never consulted. And because we were never consulted we have no need to defend the decisions or ideas that have produced over 50,000 nuclear warheads. We say "no" to this obscenity. And we say "yes" to the fresh ideas and alternatives that people all over the world are coming up with. New ideas that will pull us away from the abyss we are all poised on.

Joanne Woodward
actress

No longer is woman's moral reasoning viewed as simply a different style; it has become a political necessity for the preservation of the world.

Dr. Dorothy Austin

It is women who can bring empathy, tolerance, insight, patience and persistence to government—the qualities we naturally have or have had to develop...women of a nation mold its morals, its religion, and its politics by the lives they live. At present, our country needs women's idealism and determination, perhaps more in politics than anywhere else.

Shirley Chisholm
former Congressperson, New York

As women, we must suggest the solutions which men haven't faced or dared to implement. We must arrive at convincing strategies to start women and men thinking in terms of peace and thus strategies to achieve lasting peace.

Lucinda Mundor

We'll turn this thing around yet!

Jane Alexander
actress

For centuries, men have left home to go to war, now women are leaving home for peace.

Greenham Women

...In the name of womanhood and of humanity, I earnestly ask that a general congress of women without limit of nationality may be appointed and held at some place deemed most convenient and at the earliest period consistent with its objects, to promote the alliance of the different nationalities, the amicable settlement of international questions, the great and general interests of peace.

Julia Ward Howe
Boston
1870

Arise, then, women of this day!
Arise all women who have hearts, whether your baptism be that of water or of tears!
Say firmly: "We will not have great questions decided by irrelevant agencies, our husbands shall not come to us, reeking with carnage, for caresses and applause,
Our sons shall not be taken from us to unlearn all that we have been able to teach them of charity, mercy and patience,
We women of one country will be too tender of those of another country to allow our sons to be trained to injure theirs."
From the bosom of the devastated earth a voice goes up with our own. It says "Disarm, Disarm!"
The sword of murder is not the balance of justice! Blood does not wipe out dishonor nor violence indicate possession. As men have often forsaken the plow and the anvil at the summons of war, let women now leave all that may be left of home for a great and earnest day of counsel.

Julia Ward Howe

Don't mourn—Organize!

Joe Hill

Don't agonize. Organize.

Florynce Kennedy

The future depends on what we do in the present.

Mahatma Gandhi

Think through the problem to take back control of your future from those who are only concerned with their present.   **David Durenberger
Senator, Minnesota
speech to high school students**

We cannot wait for the world to turn, for times to change that we might change with them, for the revolution to come and carry us around in its new course. We ourselves are the future. We are the revolution.

**Beatrice Bruteau
philosopher**

Peace is our work....To everyone, Christians, believers, and men and women of good will, I say: do not be afraid to take a chance on peace, to teach peace....Peace will be the last word of history.

Pope John Paul II

Peace is positive, and it has to be waged with all our thought, energy, and courage and with the conviction that war is not inevitable.

**Dean Acheson
former Secretary of State**

The major task that good persons should set themselves to is to teach others to say no.

Pierre J. Proudhon
1858

We have seen how the vicious circle of the war system feeds on itself: distrust breeds distrust; hostility generates (and seems to justify) hostility. We forget that the benign circle of building real security is far more potent. The explosive chain reaction of peacemaking is something we rarely consider, yet I believe it will happen. Only when we see it happening will we look back and say, "If only we had known then that it was possible."

Wendy Mogey

It is the depth of the crisis that empowers hope. The power of turning, that radically changes the situation, never reveals itself outside of crisis.

Martin Buber

Ronald Reagan says we have a "window of vulnerability" and need more nuclear weapons. I see the Nuclear Freeze campaign as a "window of opportunity."

James Oberstar
Congressperson, Minnesota

* If men can develop weapons that are so terrifying as to make the thought of global war include almost a sentence for suicide, you would think that man's intelligence and his comprehension...would include also his ability to find a peaceful solution.

Dwight D. Eisenhower

* What has been spoiled through men's fault can be made good again through men's work.

I Ching

War is an invention of the human mind. The human mind can invent peace with justice.

Norman Cousins

* Since war begins in the minds of men, it is in the minds of men that peace must be constructed.

UNESCO Constitution

It was a thought that built this whole portentous war establishment, and a thought shall melt it away.

Ralph Waldo Emerson

Take an ecologically fragile planet with scarce resources and a growing population and we have a recipe for human conflict. Add conventional weapons—a recipe for war. Add nuclear weapons—a recipe for holocaust. This is our challenge as a species. But we are not without resources. Add human intelligence, knowledge, ingenuity, problem-solving skills. Add a deep value commitment to peace, to the common good. Add the spiritual tradition of humanity. We are equal to the task. But we must prepare, educate and train ourselves to be peacemakers.

Northland College
Peace Studies Department

...We have extraordinary mental equipment for the task [of evolving past nuclear weapons]—equipment we are only beginning to mobilize on behalf of the...individual and collective change required for survival.

Robert Jay Lifton and Richard Falk
Indefensible Weapons

The possibilities for tomorrow are usually beyond our expectations.

Anonymous

Can we eliminate the institution of war? The institutions of war and slavery entered history at about the same point as agricultural societies were emerging. They need to leave history at about the same point.

Yvonne V. Delk
Office for Church in Society
United Church of Christ

Many people justify war because the Bible says there will be wars and rumors of war. The Bible also talks about slavery. But we have abolished slavery. The new abolitionists will abolish war and poverty.

Anonymous

It is human will, operating under social forces, that has abolished slavery, infanticide, duelling, and a score of other social enormities. Why should it not do the same for war?

John Haynes Holmes

Though previous generations were also inspired by the fervent will to improve the world, they failed because they did not call a final halt to the forces of destruction. To do this is precisely the task of the present generation...

Queen Juliana
of the Netherlands

The basic terms of the nuclear arms race were set down 40 years ago, and since then the debate has barely changed. Generations of political leaders have failed to come to terms with the fundamental issues of nuclear terror. Today things are changing. With the example and encouragement of groups such as Physicians for Social Responsibility, citizens are becoming willing to assert their own expertise and power over nuclear questions. This is essential for the future of all of us, and of all of tomorrow's children.

Anthony S. Earl
Governor, Wisconsin

The Roman Catholic Bishops' pastoral letter on war and peace is a prophetic statement which challenges current nuclear policies and directions and democratizes the nuclear debate. It may well mark a turning point toward Einstein's new way of thinking, the paradigm shift which turns us from the prospect of nuclear holocaust to a safer world.

Major General Kermit D. Johnson
retired Army Chief of Chaplains

We are not haunted so much by events as by our beliefs about them, the crippling self-image we take with us. We can transform the present and future by reawakening the powerful past, with its recurrent message of defeat. We can face the crossroads again. We can rechoose. In a similar spirit, we can respond differently to the tragedies of modern history. Our past is not our potential. In any hour, with all the stubborn teachers and healers of history who called us to our best selves, we can liberate the future. One by one, we can re-choose—to awaken. To leave the prison of our conditioning, to love, to turn homeward. To conspire with and for each other. Awakening brings its own assignments, unique to each of us, chosen by each of us. Whatever you may think about yourself and however long you may have thought it, you are not just you. You are a seed, a silent promise. You are the conspiracy.

Marilyn Ferguson
The Aquarian Conspiracy

Before water turns to ice, it looks just the same as before. Then a few crystals form, and suddenly the whole system undergoes cataclysmic change.

Joanna Rogers Macy

Where there is a will for peace, there is a way for us working together to have it.

Jeanne Larson

If I could have 3 wishes, world peace would be all three.

Marlia Moore
8th Grader

* In the face of the man-made calamity that every war is, one must affirm and reaffirm, again and again, that the waging of war is *not* inevitable or unchangeable. Humanity is not destined to self destruction. Clashes of ideologies, aspirations and needs can and must be settled and resolved by means other than war and violence.

Pope John Paul II

I would guess there is at least an 85 percent certainty that humanity will wipe itself out in the reasonably near future—but I put my faith in the remaining 15 percent.

Leo Szilard
early atomic scientist

I have to cast my lot with those who age after age, with no extraordinary power, reconstitute the world.

Adrienne Rich

In the final analysis, the best guarantee that a thing should happen is that it appears to us as vitally necessary.

Pierre Teilhard de Chardin

It is necessary; therefore, it is possible.

G. A. Borghese

It is absolutely realistic in that we have to do it. We have to learn to resolve conflict without war or die, along with the rest of life on the planet. It is the people who still believe war is still an alternative who are dealing in fantasy.

Regina Roney
Beyond War Project

Nonviolent action, seeking just structures and also a conversion of attitude involving the entire human society...is a practical way of choosing life over death.

International Fellowship of Reconciliation

* The brontosaurus became extinct, but it wasn't its fault, so to speak. If we become extinct, it will be our fault....in order to survive, man has to evolve.

And to evolve, we need a new kind of thinking and a new kind of behavior, a new ethic and a new morality. It will be that of the evolution of everyone rather than the survival of the fittest.

In terms of evolutionary behavior, that means choosing at each moment to adopt the attitudes and values—cooperation, caring, loving, forgiving—that are absolutely essential if we are not to destroy ourselves.

It's not easy, but it's worth every difficulty.

There is nothing mushy, vague or soft-headed about loving and forgiving. In fact, the end result would be to release the power in the nucleus of each individual—a power much greater in its positive effects than atomic power is in its negative. **Jonas Salk**
Parade
November 1984

We will love one another or we will die.

Jehan Sadat

We must erase the lines that keep us from peace.

Erin Troy
4th Grader

If we would see peace flowering in the world tomorrow we must plant the seeds of love today.

Anonymous

We have continuously to repeat, although it is a voice that cries in the desert, "No to violence, yes to peace."

Bishop Oscar Romero
El Salvador

E. Challenge to the Nation

Dear Mr. President:
Please don't have a war even if you get mad at the Russians. My mother always tells me that if I get mad at somebody I should count to ten first.

Bennett K.
Cincinnati, Age 9
Please Save My World

A wiser rule would be to make up your mind soberly what you want, peace or war, and then to get ready for what you want; for what we prepare for is what we shall get.

William Graham Sumner
War

If the State wishes that its citizens respect human life, then the State should stop killing.

Clarence Darrow

There mustn't be any more war. It disturbs too many people.

French peasant woman

* Will allegiance to the fatal ideal of national sovereignty be transferred to the ideal of world government in time to save mankind from self-destruction?

Arnold Toynbee

I think arms control and the United Nations are good ideas, but I don't think they can work unless the governments want them to work. And I don't think governments want them to work.

Lena Flores
Age 17
Our Future at Stake

Business people who succeed know that when the survival of their enterprise is threatened, they must change course. As influential shareholders in our national enterprise, business leaders must mandate our management—our employees in government—to stop and reverse the nuclear arms race. We must tell them: Find a way. Come up with a plan. It can be done. It must be done. Do it.

Harold Willens
business executive

...the only way to handle the enormous problems of the arms race is to get on with the job of disarmament itself.

Arthur Lall

I hear some people say that it would take a miracle to put peace in the world, but it wouldn't. If the two presidents would talk together, it would work out all right.

6th Grader

Bombs can't tell anybody how they're feeling, they'll have to talk themselves, not war it.

6th Grader

...I wish Reagan and Andropov could just sit down and talk without TV cameras and without interpreters and just talk like two human beings.

Wenonah Elms
Age 13
Our Future at Stake

When I went to preschool the teachers told me to always talk a problem out with a friend instead of fighting. I've often thought of that when people speak of war. I don't see why people have to fight like they do.

Heather Prior
7th Grader

I mean, if we could be friends by just getting to know each other better, then what are our countries really arguing about? Nothing could be more important than not having a war if a war would kill everything.

Samantha Smith
Age 10
letter to Andropov on returning
from the Soviet Union at his invitation

If nations could overcome the mutual fear and distrust whose somber shadow is now thrown over the world, and could meet with confidence and good will to settle their possible differences, they would easily be able to establish a lasting peace.

Fridtjof Nansen

...Down the long lane of history yet to be written America knows that this world of ours, ever growing smaller, must avoid becoming a community of dreadful fear and hate, and be, instead, a proud confederation of mutual trust and respect....Disarmament, with mutual honor and confidence, is a continuing imperative. Together we must learn how to compose differences, not with arms, but with intellect and decent purpose.

Dwight D. Eisenhower

More than an end to war, we want an end to the beginnings of all wars—yes, an end to this brutal, inhuman and thoroughly impractical method of settling the differences between governments.

Franklin Delano Roosevelt

If they want peace, nations should avoid the pin-pricks that precede cannon-shots.

Napoleon Bonaparte

Why do we invest all our skills and resources in a contest for armed superiority which can never be attained for long enough to make it worth having, rather than in an effort to find a *modus vivendi* with our antagonist—that is to say, a way of living, not dying?

Barbara Tuchman
The March of Folly—From Troy to Vietnam

The time has come when we must ask our leaders to find new ways to settle conflicts. If we put as much time, energy and money into peace as we do into weapons of destruction, there is no question but that we would find new solutions.

Betty Bumpers
founder of Peace Links

They are talking about basing modes instead of basics. Why does the arms race go on? Why, if we can negotiate a wheat deal, can't we negotiate a reduction in nuclear weapons? If we don't, we could end up in a world where there will be nobody to grow the wheat and nobody to eat the bread.

Mary McGrory
October 1981

There is no practical problem existing between nations whose importance is in any proportion to the tremendous losses which must be expected in an atomic war.

Albert Schweitzer
***Teaching of Reverence for Life*, 1965**

If peace is the overriding concern of the human race, we ought to be willing to bend our best energies and intellect to a consideration of how the ethical insights of each nation are translated into a charter of peace for all nations.

Earl Warren
former Chief Justice
U.S. Supreme Court

Is it too much to hope that what is made possible for just a couple of days by the occurrence of common holidays, may soon prove feasible for a longer period by the new commitments that peace requires, so that an atmosphere may be created which is necessary for meaningful talks to be held in the quest for a peaceful solution?

U Thant
former Secretary-General, UN

Let us never negotiate out of fear, but let us never fear to negotiate.

John F. Kennedy

I have said time and again there is no place on this earth to which I would not travel; there is no chore I would not undertake if I had any faintest hope that, by so doing, I would promote the general cause of world peace.

Dwight D. Eisenhower

* Never have the nations of the world had so much to lose or so much to gain. Together we shall save our planet or together we shall perish in its flames. Save it we can and save it we must, and then shall we earn the eternal thanks of mankind and, as peacemakers, the eternal blessing of God.

John F. Kennedy

Let us take the risks of peace upon our lives, not impose the risks of war upon the world.

Quaker proverb

We call upon governments to accept risks of peace rather than to impose upon us and our children the certainties that grow out of massive preparations for war.

Fellowship of Reconciliation

To break this mad cycle we call for bold and creative initiatives such as a unilateral decision by our government to terminate all nuclear tests and the production of all nuclear weapons and their delivery systems. In turn, we appeal to the Soviet Union to reciprocate in order to halt the rush toward a nuclear holocaust.

Church of the Brethren
Annual Conference resolution, 1980

The U.S. having led in the development of nuclear power should also lead in its effective utilization and control...

Episcopal Church
General Convention resolution
1976

* The country that adopts a policy of total disarmament, without waiting for its neighbors, will be able to lead the world away from hatred, fear, and mistrust towards the true community, the harmony of man.

Mahatma Gandhi

The world waits for a great nation that has the common sense, the imagination, and the faith to devote to the science and practice of nonviolence so much as a tenth of the money, brains, skill and devotion which it now devotes to the madness of war preparation. What is that nation waiting for before it undertakes its mission?

A. J. Muste

The greatest honor history can bestow is the title of peacemaker. This honor now beckons America....This is our summons to greatness.

Richard M. Nixon

God and the politicians willing, the United States can declare peace upon the world, and win it.

Ely Culbertson

ADDITIONS:

ADDITIONS:

26
Peace Conversion

The Defense Department cannot and should not assume responsibility for creating or maintaining levels of economic activity.

Policy Declarations
U.S. Chamber of Commerce
1975

We know too that vast armaments are arising on every side and that the work of creating them employs men and women by the millions. It is natural, however, for us to conclude that such employment is false employment, that it builds no permanent structures and creates no consumers' goods for the maintenance of a lasting prosperity. We know that nations guilty of these follies inevitably face the day when either their weapons of destruction must be used against their neighbors or when an unsound economy like a house of cards will fall apart.

Franklin D. Roosevelt
December 1936

The idea of planned economic conversion means a redirection of the scientific and technical talent now concentrated in military production. There are many who attribute the faltering U.S. economy to the fact that nearly half of all our scientists and engineers are employed in the defense sector. If their numbers were redeployed to research and development in the civilian sector, the United States could regain its once dynamic role in the world economy.

Anonymous

Next spring, almost one-third of the bright young engineers graduating from the Massachusetts Institute of Technology will take jobs designing weapons.

Rick Atkinson and Fred Hiatt

I wonder what the engineers, technicians, and workers who make weapons all day long for killing their neighbor can possibly be thinking of. They're not working for a living; they're working for dying.

Adolfo Pérez Esquivel
1980 Nobel Peace Prize
Christ in a Poncho

We can no longer afford—socially or financially—to support irresponsible companies that endanger the very future we are investing for.

Susan Meeker-Lowry
co-editor, *Good Money: A Newsletter of Social Investing*

More and more people are beginning to "put their money where their heart is," which is the basic premise behind what is called social or ethical investing.

Susan Meeker-Lowry
co-editor, *Good Money: A Newsletter of Social Investing*

If the goal is to provide jobs and employment opportunities, then almost any category of non-military employment will produce more work for one billion dollars than does defense production.

U.S. Department of Labor

Many people assume that military spending is necessary to create jobs. In fact, however, defense production is one of the least effective means of providing employment. As military production has become more capital intensive and automated, the volume of employment has dropped. Military spending also accelerates inflation and hinders the development of civilian technology.

Anonymous

We know that the roller coaster cycle of defense production does not provide us with economic and job security....Planned economic conversion is the humane way, the sensible way, the only way to get workers, communities, and even entire states off the dependency hook.

William Winpisinger
President, International Association
of Machinists and Aerospace Workers

* I think it is a terrible thing for a human being to feel that his security and the well-being of his family hinge upon a continuation of the insanity of the arms race. We have to give these people greater economic security in terms of the rewarding purposes of peace.

Walter Reuther
labor leader
1969

We believe we can convert our industries to meet human needs....We do not have to choose between protecting our jobs and protecting our lives!

Women's Peace Presence

...we call upon the President...and Congress...to seek seriously the development of peaceful ways to resolve conflicts between nations and to plan expeditiously for conversion to a healthy economy based on production for nonmilitary purposes.

The Christian Church
(Disciples of Christ)
resolution "Concerning Ending the Arms Race"
1979

We are all too familiar with community outcries when a military base is threatened with closure. Yet forty-eight bases which have been closed now house seven four-year colleges, twenty-six technical institutes, six vocational schools, and a variety of other educational centers with a total student enrollment of 62,000.

Anonymous

The nuclear industry has developed to become an industry of narrow specialists, each promoting and refining a fragment of the technology, with little comprehension of the total impact on our world system....We [resigned] because we could no longer justify devoting our life energies to the continued development and expansion of nuclear fission power—a system we believe to be so dangerous that it now threatens the very existence of life on this planet.

Dale Bridenbaugh, Richard Hubbard and Gregory Minor
Nuclear Engineers, General Electric Company

My reason for leaving G.E. is a deep conviction that nuclear reactors and nuclear weapons now present a serious danger for the future of all life on this planet. I am convinced that the reactors, the nuclear fuel cycle, and waste storage systems are not safe.

Gregory Minor
former Manager, Advanced Control, G.E.

I do not want you or anyone to be put out of work. That would not be peace. Peace is where people can work in similar jobs but no one will have to do work connected to nuclear weapons or military communications.

Jeanne Larson
to engineer at ELF facility

We want our country's use of money and minds *redirected* from inventing ways to destroy one another to learning how to *live* together.

Women's Peace Presence

We make a living by what we get, but we make a life by what we give.

Winston Churchill

Our life is more than our work; our work is more than our jobs.

Charlie King
from the song "More Than Our Work"

The highest reward for toil is not what you get for it but what you become by it.

John Ruskin

27
Encouragement for
Peace Workers

Every noble work is at first impossible.

Thomas Carlyle

All truth passes through three stages.
First, it is ridiculed.
Second, it is violently opposed.
Third, it is accepted as being self-evident.

Schopenhauer

Beware of:
  Justification of procrastination
  Paralysis of analysis.

Martin Luther King, Jr.

It is better to have inadequate answers to relevant questions rather than sophisticated answers to obsolete questions.

Action Linkage

We sometimes fall into the delusion that power is elsewhere, that it belongs to a different group, that we are unable to find access to it. Nothing could be further from the truth. The universe oozes with power, waiting for anyone who wishes to embrace it. But because the powers of cosmic dynamics are invisible, we need to remind ourselves of their universal presence. Who reminds us? The rivers, plains, galaxies, hurricanes, lightning branches and all our living companions.

Brian Swimme
The Universe Is a Green Dragon

* He who molds public sentiment goes deeper than he who enacts statutes or pronounces decisions. He makes statutes or decisions possible or impossible to make.

Abraham Lincoln

Caring about the world doesn't begin with fear or morbidity but with fascination.

Garrison Keillor

Nothing in life is to be feared, it is only to be understood.

Marie Curie

Survivalists arm and retreat—they will only die. We are the survivalists—those of us who disarm and reach out our arms to others.

Anonymous

* Of every invention, of every organization, of every fresh political or economic proposal, we must dare to demand: Has it been conceived in love and does it further the long-term purposes of man? Much that we do would not survive such a question. But much that is still open to man's creative acts of self-transformation would at last become possible. Not power but power directed by love into the forms of beauty and truth is what we need for our survival, to say nothing of our further development. Only when love takes the lead will the earth, and life on earth, be safe again. And not until then.

Lewis Mumford
The Opening Future

They call us radicals but there is nothing more radical than nuclear war. In fact, we are the conservatives bent on saving the planet.

Anonymous

The job of the peacemaker is to stop war, to purify the world, to get it saved from poverty and riches, to heal the sick, to comfort the sad, to wake up those who have not yet found God, to create beauty and joy wherever you go, to find God in everything and everybody.

Muriel Lester

To find the way to make peace with ourselves and to offer it to others, both spiritually and politically, is the most important kind of learning. To accept our abilities and limitations, and the differences of others; this is the contentment that gives life its highest value. It frees us to grow without restraint and to settle without pressure.

Wendy C. Schwartz

* ..there is a pervasive form of contemporary violence to which the idealist fighting for peace by nonviolent methods most easily succumbs: activism and overwork. The rush and pressure of modern life are a form, perhaps the most common form, of its innate violence. To allow oneself to be carried away by a multitude of conflicting concerns, to surrender to too many demands, to commit oneself to too many projects, to want to help everyone in everything is to succumb to violence. More than that, it is cooperation in violence. The frenzy of the activist neutralizes his work for peace. It destroys his own inner capacity for peace. It destroys the fruitfulness of his own work, because it kills the root of inner wisdom which makes work fruitful.

Thomas Merton

* He who attempts to act and do things for others or for the world without deepening his own self-understanding, freedom, integrity and capacity to love, will not have anything to give others. He will communicate to them nothing but the contagion of his own obsessions, his aggressiveness, his ego-centered ambitions, his delusions about ends and means, his doctrinaire prejudices and ideas.

Thomas Merton

We must have a flaming moral purpose so that greed, oppression and exploitation shrivel before the fire within you.

graffito in South Minneapolis
Indian neighborhood

Bull Connor would next say, "Turn the fire hoses on." And as I said before, Bull Connor didn't know history. He knew a kind of physics that somehow didn't relate to the transphysics that we were about. And that was the fact that there was a certain kind of fire no water could put out.

Martin Luther King, Jr.

---

* Liberty lies in the hearts of men; when it dies there, no law, no jury, no judge can save it.

Judge Learned Hand

* Liberty lies in the hearts of men; when it exists there, no law, no jury, no judge can destroy it.

David Samas
Fort Hood Three
We Won't Go

To avoid burnout (a state of mental distress or apathy, not to be confused with simply getting tired):
1) We must not take ourselves too seriously (although the things we care about are serious issues),
2) We must recognize we can only do as well as we can and no more, and
3) Laugh a lot—at yourself, the world and with others.

Madge Micheels-Cyrus

Let me tell you the secret that has led me to my goal. My strength lies solely in my tenacity.

Louis Pasteur

The fight must go on. The cause of civil liberty must not be surrendered at the end of one or even one hundred defeats.

Abraham Lincoln

People say, what is the sense of our small effort. They cannot see that we must lay one brick at a time, take one step at a time.

Dorothy Day

* When nothing seems to help, I go and look at a stonecutter hammering away at his rock perhaps a hundred times without as much as a crack showing in it. Yet at the hundred and first blow it will split in two, and I know it was not that blow that did it—but all that had gone before.

Jacob Riis

The power of ideals is incalculable. We see no power in a drop of water. But let it get into a crack in the rock and be turned to ice, and it splits the rock.

Albert Schweitzer

* When you begin a great work you can't expect to finish it all at once; therefore, do you and your brothers press on, and let nothing discourage you...

Teedyuscung
Delaware Tribe
1758

When you get into a tight place and everything goes against you, till it seems as though you could not hold on a minute longer, never give up then, for that is just the place and time that the tide will turn.

Harriet Beecher Stowe

I still believe that we shall overcome. This faith can give us courage to face the uncertainties of the future. It will give our tired feet new strength as we continue our forward stride toward the city of freedom. When our days become dreary with low-hovering clouds and our nights become darker than a thousand midnights, we will know that we are living in the creative turmoil of a genuine civilization struggling to be born...

Martin Luther King, Jr.
on receiving the Nobel Peace Prize

Courage is the price that life exacts for granting peace.

Amelia Earhart

Civic courage, as we call it in time of peace, is the kind of valor to which the monuments of nations should most of all be raised.

William James

A rabbi (who lived and preached a life of virtue while his congregation ignored him and went on with their selfish ways) was asked: "Rabbi, why do you bother? Nobody listens. You're not changing anything." And the rabbi replied: "But you misunderstand. I don't do it to change them. I do it to keep them from changing me."

Anonymous

I'm not trying to change the world. I'm trying to keep the world from changing me.

Ammon Hennacy

In other words we have to push against the walls to find out where they really are. The other reason we have to push is that if we do not push them out, they push us in.

John Holt

* There are moments when things go well and one feels encouraged. There are difficult moments and one feels overwhelmed. But it's senseless to speak of optimism or pessimism. The only important thing is to know that if one works well in a potato field, the potatoes will grow. If one works well among men, they will grow—that's reality. The rest is smoke. It's important to know that words don't move mountains. Work, exacting work, moves mountains.

Danilo Dolci

Perhaps it is an idle task to judge in times when action counts.

Albert Einstein

Actions are clearly effective when those involved in them experience their capabilities and their strength. That exciting feeling of empowerment is something that cannot be taken away. It becomes part of how we think about ourselves, as purposeful, effective people who can express ourselves clearly on an issue of vital importance.

Greenham Women Everywhere

Jesus asks us to speak for peace whether or not it is effective in the worldly sense. The whole question is the question of faithfulness, and not just the question of change....So in the middle of this world we need to say "no" to war even when we don't see immediate results. In the Second World War when the Jews were all being gassed, lots of us didn't do or say anything, because we said we couldn't do anything about it. But those who did speak and act, without success, are still celebrated as people who gave history hope.

Henri Nouwen

* We who lived in concentration camps can remember the men who walked through the huts comforting others, giving away their last piece of bread. They may have been few in number, but they offer sufficient proof that everything can be taken from a man but one thing: the last of the human freedoms—to choose one's attitude in any given set of circumstances— to choose one's own way.

Viktor Frankl

* God has not called me to be successful. He has called me to be faithful.

Mother Teresa

An act of love that fails is just as much a part of the divine life as an act of love that succeeds, for love is measured by its own fullness not by its reception.

Harold Loukes

We must approach the job of creating a peaceful world with the discipline and patience of a fine gardener. We make our plans, we break the ground and prepare it to receive our seeds. We work with the cycles of growth and weather. At times we work hard, sweating in teams; at other times we quietly repair our tools in solitude. Some of our crops are fast- growing and nourish us sooner than other ones will. The flowers give us beauty and joy throughout the season. We do a little every day, and we know that after a long period of tending and growth, a lovely harvest is coming.

Mary Hayes-Grieco

...for every gardener knows that after the digging, after the planting, after the long season of tending and growth, the harvest comes.

Marge Piercy
The Influence Coming into Play: The Seven of Pentacles

In the struggle rewards are few
In fact I know of only two
Loving friends and living dreams
These rewards are not so few it seems

Anonymous

I have no political analysis of resistance to offer that justifies hope. We have to expect the worst, for a while. But I know from the tradition that sustains the struggling and suffering people...that terror will not have the last word.

Dorothee Sölle

Hope is not the lucky gift of circumstance or disposition, but a virtue like faith and love, to be practiced whether or not we find it easy or even natural, because it is necessary to our survival as human beings.

Clara Park
The Siege

Hope is a waking dream.   **Anonymous**

Hope is that thing with feathers that perches in the soul and sings the tune without the words and never stops at all.

Emily Dickinson

No peace lies in the future which is not hidden in the present instant.
Take peace.
The gloom of the world is but a shadow;
Behind it, yet within reach, is joy.
Take joy.

Fra Giovani
1513

If I can't dance...I don't want to be part of your revolution.

Emma Goldman

A movement is when people do all the things they sing about.

James Bevel

I'd rather vote for something I want and not get it than vote for something I don't want, and get it.

Eugene V. Debs

Say I was a drum major for justice, I was a drum major for peace, I was a drum major for righteousness, say that I left a committed life behind...

Martin Luther King, Jr.

The future does not belong to those who are content with today. Rather it will belong to those who can blend vision, reason and courage in a personal commitment.

Robert F. Kennedy

The fabric of the new society will be made of nothing more or less than the threads woven in today's interactions.

Pam McAllister
Reweaving the Web of Life

They never die, who have the future in them.

Meridel Le Sueur

ADDITIONS:

28
Role of Imaging in Peace Work

A mind that is stretched by a new idea can never go back to its original dimensions.

Oliver Wendell Holmes

You may say I'm a dreamer, but I'm not the only one.

John Lennon

A person without dreams is standing still. A state without dreams is standing still. A nation without dreams is standing still.

Paul Simon
Senator, Illinois

Where there is no vision, the people perish.

Proverbs 29:18a
King James Version

With compass, the mariner is able to navigate regardless of the nature of the craft or the conditions of the weather. With a theory that lets us see—we can perceive what is at work in us, through us, and for us in this planet-time. It helps us to stay steady and sure. Without it, we risk the extremes of being locked in numbness or swept away by panic as we open to the magnitude of the dangers confronting us.

Joanna Rogers Macy
Despair and Personal Power in the Nuclear Age

Twentieth century humans have lost their capacity to visualize a future different from the present, and that only by reconstituting our visioning capacity can we make any meaningful future possible for the human race.

Fred Polak
Image of the Future

I believe that focussing on what the social order might look like if we handled conflict without weapons is a critical part of the task of imaging any future at all.

Elise Boulding

We have actually forgotten that every civilization has had its vision of the world as a peaceable garden, with abundance for all, a garden without weapons....That vision is the oldest and most persistently recurring vision in human experience. And yet today we cannot even visualize what a disarmed world would look like.

Elise Boulding
1981

In our striving for peace in the 1980s, we have looked too much to Washington, Moscow, Geneva, Vienna...and too little to *ourselves*. It is not only a failure of arms control negotiations that keeps peace from being a reality in our time but also a failure of our *own imaginations*.

Waging Peace

I am not proposing a static utopian depiction for the peace movement. I am suggesting that we return to a long forgotten tradition of visualizing the good society and exploring what the visualizations themselves might teach us about strategies for the present.

Elise Boulding

Only when we can in some sense visualize a world without weapons can we find the path to it....What happens as the result of this kind of work is that we perceive connections that we normally do not see. We develop images of strategies we have never thought of.

Elise Boulding

The images just are. Let them come to you. See where they will take you into a world without war. This is adventure, this is journey, this is discovery.

Warren Ziegler

Fantasies are more than substitutes for unpleasant reality; they are also dress rehearsals, plans. All acts performed in the world begin in the imagination.

Barbara Harrison

Imagination is more important than knowledge.

Albert Einstein

* Nothing ever built arose to touch the skies unless some man dreamed that it should, some man believed that it could, and some man willed that it must.

Charles Kettering
past President
General Motors Research Corporation

In planning for a future of peace, there are no experts to lead us. There are no colleges to train us. The inventions will arise from our deep longing, our imagination, our hopes, our common sense. We can start building a peaceful future by first creating images of it in our minds.

Women's Peace Presence

* Anything that a man can dream, a man can do.

John Lily
Center of the Cyclone

What you can imagine, you can create.

Anonymous

For tomorrow is what we make it, and it will be ours.

The Mothers of the Plaza de Mayo
Argentina, July 1980
Christ in a Poncho

...The wild dream is the first step to reality by which we set our highest goals and discern our highest selves.

Norman Cousins

Most advocates of realism in this world are hopelessly unrealistic.

Jawaharlal Nehru

* I refuse to accept the idea that the "isness" of man's present nature makes him morally incapable of reaching up for the "oughtness" that forever confronts him.

Martin Luther King, Jr.

Other people see things and say why—but I dream things that never were and say why not?

George Bernard Shaw

* Some men see things as they are and ask why. I dream things that never were and ask why not.

Robert F. Kennedy

Beware what you set your heart upon for it surely shall be yours.

Ralph Waldo Emerson

What we call non-existent is what we do not desire enough.

Nikos Kazantzakis

What you can do, or dream you can, begin it. Boldness has genius, power, and magic in it.

Goethe

Societies generate images of the possible and then draw their behavior from those images.

Elise Boulding

The paradigm of the *Aquarian Conspiracy* sees humankind embedded in nature. It promotes the autonomous individual in a decentralized society. It sees us as stewards of all our resources, inner and outer. It says that we are not victims, not pawns, not limited by conditions or conditioning. Heirs to evolutionary riches, we are capable of imagination, invention, and experience we have only glimpsed.

Marilyn Ferguson
The Aquarian Conspiracy

...by asking our help you recognize that connection; and...we are reminded of other connections that lie far deeper than the facts on the surface...to discuss with you the capacity of the human spirit to overflow boundaries and make unity out of multiplicity. But that would be to dream—to dream the recurring dream that has haunted the human mind since the beginning of time; the dream of peace, the dream of freedom. But with the sound of guns in your ears you have not asked us to dream. You have not asked us what peace is; you have asked us to prevent war...not by repeating your words and following your methods but by finding new words and creating new methods.

Virginia Woolf
Three Guineas

The future is not a result of choices among alternative paths offered by the present, but a place that is created—created first in the mind and will, created next in activity. The future is not some place we are going to but one we are creating. The paths are not to be found, but made, and the activity of making them changes both the maker and the destination.

John Schaar

We cannot discover new oceans unless we have the courage to lose sight of the shore.

Anonymous

Think about the kind of world you want to live and work in. What do you need to know to build the world? Demand that your teachers teach you that.

Kropotkin

Imagine, imagine, that whatever you see can come true...
Imagine, imagine—just as long as what you see you do!

Susan Savell

You are never given a wish without also being given the power to make it true. You may have to work for it, however.

Richard Bach

In hope against all human hope...Faith, mighty faith, the promise sees and looks to that alone; laughs at impossibilities. And cries, "It shall be done."

Anonymous

It's fun to do the impossible.

Walt Disney

I ask myself, is it just a wild flight of imagination to conceive of a world without war...but someone must try...

Julia Grace Wales

One of the things in which women are vitally interested to-day is the abolition of war as a means of settling disputes between nations, and I feel that this is particularly a question which is up to the women...The will to peace will have to start with women and they will have to want peace sufficiently to be crusaders on the subject. Joan of Arc, who was only a simple peasant girl, had a vision of how she could lead her country through victorious war to freedom. The women of to-day must have a vision of how to lead the world to peace.

Eleanor Roosevelt
1933

It is a peculiar fact of life for those of us alive today...that without a near-future breakthrough into a true realization of our familyhood, there will be no future generations. Let us envision utopia, and thus bring it into existence. There is no reasonable alternative.

Dr. Willis Harman
regent, University of California

What we want to change is immense. It's not just getting rid of nuclear weapons, it's getting rid of the whole structure that created the possibility of nuclear weapons in the first place. If we don't use imagination nothing will change. Without change we will destroy the planet. It's as simple as that.

Lesley Boulton
Greenham Common
1982

ADDITIONS:

29
Visions of Peace

A. Peace Is/Is Not

B. Old Testament Images of Peace

C. Peace Is Possible

D. Images of Government
   in a Peaceful World

E. Beyond War

Let the people take heart and hope everywhere, for the cross is bending,
the midnight is passing, and joy cometh with the morning.
Eugene Debs

We grow toward the light, not toward darkness.
Ashley Montagu

The dark night is over and dawn has begun,
Rise, hope of the ages arise like the sun!
All speech flow to music, all hearts beat as one.
John Greenleaf Whittier

No war, or battle's sound
Was heard the world around.
The idle spear and shield were high up hung.
John Milton
On the Morning of Christ's Nativity

A. Peace Is/Is Not

There is no way to peace, peace is the way.
A. J. Muste

Peace is a spirit, and not an intellectual abstraction: it is a life, not a theory.
Elihu Burritt
1846

Peace is like a plant, growing with the care of a human being.
Lance Schellin
9th Grader

Peace is like a newborn baby, waiting to be noticed by the world.
Melissa Naumann
9th Grader

...peace is neither the absence of war nor the presence of a disarmament
agreement. Peace is a change of heart.
Richard D. Lamm
Governor, Colorado

Peace is people talking together with a heart in between them.
Child
Age 8

Peace is the countries of the world coming together to be one in friendship.
Katie Hisrich
7th Grader

Go down to the foot of the mountain; throw away your gun, your ammunition, your provisions, and your clothing; wash yourself in the stream which flows there, and you will then be prepared to stand before the Master of Life.

Pontiac
Ottawa
1763

The thickness of your skin will be seven spans, for you will be proof against anger, offensive action, and criticism. With endless patience you shall carry out your duty, and your firmness shall be tempered with compassion for your people. Neither anger nor fear shall find lodgement in your mind, and all your words and actions will be tempered with calm deliberation. In all your official acts, self-interest shall be cast aside. You shall look and listen to the welfare of the whole people, and have always in view, not only the present but the coming generations—the unborn of the future Nation.

Dekanawidah
to leaders of the Iroquois Confederation

Peace is a maze, winding and twisting to find a way out of confusion and blackness.

Andy Hagan
9th Grader

Lead me from death to life, from falsehood to truth.
Lead me from despair to hope, from fear to trust.
Lead me from hate to love, from war to peace.
Let peace fill our heart, our world, our universe.

World Peace Prayer

Peace is not an absence of war, it is a virtue, a state of mind, a disposition for benevolence, confidence, justice.

Benedict Spinoza

We realize that the peace we enjoy is the absence of war, rather than the presence of confidence, understanding and generous conduct.

Raymond G. Swing

We are changing because we must. Historically, peace efforts have been aimed at ending or preventing wars. Just as we have defined health in negative terms, as the absence of disease, we have defined peace as non-conflict. But peace is more fundamental than that. Peace is a state of mind, not a state of the nation. Without personal transformation, the people of the world will be forever locked in conflict. If we limit ourselves to the old-paradigm concept of averting war, we are trying to overpower darkness rather than switching on the light. If we reframe the problem—if we think of fostering community health, innovation, self-discovery, purpose—we are already engaged in waging peace. In a rich, creative, meaningful environment there is no room for hostility. War is unthinkable in a society of autonomous people who have discovered the connectedness of all humanity, who are unafraid of alien ideas and alien cultures, who know that all revolutions begin within and that you cannot impose your brand of enlightenment on anyone else.

Marilyn Ferguson
The Aquarian Conspiracy

Consider the history of America closely. Never has America lost a war....But name, if you can, the last peace the United States won. Victory yes, but this country has never made a successful peace because peace requires exchanging ideas, concepts, thoughts, and recognizing the fact that two distinct systems of life can exist together without conflict...

Vine Deloria, Jr.
I Have Spoken
1969

It must be peace without victory...Victory would mean peace forced upon the loser, a victor's terms imposed upon the vanquished. It would be accepted in humiliation, under duress, at an intolerable sacrifice, and would leave a sting, a resentment, a bitter memory upon which terms of peace would rest, not permanently, but only as upon quicksand. Only a peace between equals can last.

Woodrow Wilson

We are living in a pre-war and not a post-war world.

Eugene Rostow
former member, US Arms Control and Disarmament Agency
June 1976

This is not peace time but a pre-war period.

Anonymous

Peace cannot be kept by force. It can only be achieved by understanding.

Albert Einstein

Peace is not only better than war, but infinitely more arduous.

George Bernard Shaw

Peace is not fighting because the world may die.

Alisa
Age 8

And is not peace, in the last analysis, basically a matter of human rights—the right to live out our lives without fear of devastation, the right to breathe air as nature provided it, the right of future generations to a healthy existence.

John F. Kennedy
1963

Peace is knowing that someone cares about me.

Kim Harshman
8th Grader

Peace is
Everyone trusting
And
Caring for
Each other.

Rachel Minshall
8th Grader

* True peace is not merely the absence of tension but is the presence of justice and brotherhood.

Martin Luther King, Jr.

* The outpouring of good sense and reason will cause men to reconsider their ways. Then, as peace settles over this earth, it is hoped people everywhere can celebrate life without fear of deadly weapons, to love instead of hate, the right to health, to earn a living, to be happy in a decent home, all things that bring about dignity.

Cleo Darmon

Peace begins when the hungry are fed.

Anonymous

They have not wanted Peace at all; they have wanted to be spared war—as though the absence of war was the same as peace. Peace is not the absence of war. Peace is a positive condition—the rule of law.

Dorothy Thompson

Peace is not the absence of conflict but the presence of creative alternatives for responding to conflict—alternatives to passive or aggressive responses, alternatives to violence.

Jeanne Larson

It is crucial that we begin to understand peace to mean, not only an end to war, but an end to all the ways we do violence to ourselves, each other, the animals, the earth.

Pam McAllister
Reweaving the Web of Life

Peace is everything living together in harmony.

Rachel Liegel
7th Grader

Peace is a chorus singing in harmony.

Jamie Hovey
9th Grader

B. Old Testament Images of Peace

...and they shall beat their swords into plowshares, and their spears into pruning hooks; nation shall not lift up sword against nation, neither shall they learn war any more.

Isaiah 2:4
RSV

The wolf shall dwell with the lamb, and the leopard shall lie down with the kid, and the calf and the lion and the fatling together, and a little child shall lead them. The cow and the bear shall feed; their young shall lie down together; and the lion shall eat straw like the ox.

Isaiah 11:6–7
RSV

And the effect of righteousness will be peace, and the result of righteousness, quietness and trust for ever. My people will abide in a peaceful habitation, in secure dwellings, and in quiet resting places.

Isaiah 32:17–18
RSV

And I will make for you a covenant on that day with the beasts of the field, the birds of the air, and the creeping things of the ground; and I will abolish the bow, the sword, and war from the land; and I will make you lie down in safety.

Hosea 2:18
RSV

C. Peace Is Possible

My song is the song of peace. We have had many war songs in my country but we have thrown them all away....I heard the voices of my ancestors crying to me in a voice of love, "My grandson, my grandson, restrain your anger; think of the living; rescue them from the fire and the knife."

Kiosaton, Iroquois Chief
1645
I Have Spoken

It seemed to me that the spirit of [my son] Hirohisa, his friends of the First Middle School who died with him, and the countless people of Hiroshima who died that day, have all gone up to the heavens and turned to stardust, and are softly looking down at us every night, so that such a catastrophe will never be repeated on earth.

Toshie Fujino

I still believe that people are really good at heart. I simply can't build up my hopes on a foundation consisting of confusion, misery and death. I see the world gradually being turned into a wilderness, I hear the ever approaching thunder, which will destroy us too. I can feel the sufferings of millions and yet, if I look up into the heavens, I think it will all come right, that this cruelty too will end, and that peace and tranquility will return again.

Anne Frank
July 1944

We will break through the layers of our denials, put aside our fainthearted excuses, and rise up to cleanse the earth of nuclear weapons.

Jonathan Schell

We shall hew out of the mountain of despair, a stone of hope.

Martin Luther King, Jr.

If someone with courage and vision can rise to lead in nonviolent action, the winter of despair can in the twinkling of an eye be turned into the summer of hope.

Mahatma Gandhi

If we all can persevere, if we can in every land and office look beyond our own shores and ambitions, then surely the age will dawn in which the strong are just and the weak secure and the peace preserved.

John F. Kennedy

I believe without a shadow of doubt that science and peace will finally triumph over ignorance and war, and that the nations of earth will ultimately agree not to destroy, but to build up.

Louis Pasteur

War is on its last legs; and a universal peace is as sure as the prevalence of civilization over barbarism, of liberal governments over feudal forms. The question for us is only—How soon?

Ralph Waldo Emerson

* When shall all men's good be each man's rule, and universal peace be like a shaft of light across the land?

Alfred Lord Tennyson

What if they gave a war and nobody came...?

Anonymous

It is possible to live in peace.

Mahatma Gandhi

* All of us—great and small, belligerents and neutrals—we must not close our ears to the dire warning of this hour, the threat of such unthinkable horrors. Peace is at hand! As a thought, a desire, a suggestion, as a power working in silence, it is everywhere, in every heart. If each one of us opens his heart to it, if each one of us firmly resolves to serve the cause of peace, to communicate his thoughts and intimations of peace—if every man of good will decides to devote himself exclusively for a little while to clearing away the obstacles, the barriers to peace, then we shall have peace.

Hermann Hesse
Shall There Be Peace?

Peace is in the air everybody can have it nobody can steal it we all can share it in the world. Peace is a special thought or a special love or light or spark that we all share within ourselves. If there was peace there would be no wars or fights just a special love all over the world.

Joel
Age 11

D. Images of Government in a Peaceful World

We, the people of the United States, in order to form a more perfect union, establish justice, insure domestic tranquility, provide for the common defense, promote the general welfare, and secure the blessings of liberty to ourselves and our posterity, do ordain and establish this Constitution for the United States of America.

Preamble to the U.S. Constitution

* We, the peoples of the United Nations, determined to save succeeding generations from the scourge of war, which twice in our lifetime has brought untold sorrow to mankind, and to reaffirm faith in fundamental human rights, in the dignity and worth of the human person, in the equal rights of men and women and of nations large and small...And for these ends to practice tolerance and live together in peace with one another as good neighbors...Have resolved to combine our efforts to accomplish these aims.

United Nations Charter

The future is international.

Anonymous

* The art of democratic government has grown from its seed in the tiny city-states of Greece to become the political mode of half the world. So let us dream of a world in which all states, great and small, work together for the peaceful flowering of the republic of man.

Adlai E. Stevenson

I am convinced that the Great Framer of the World will so develop it that it becomes one nation, so that armies and navies are no longer necessary.

Ulysses S. Grant

* We shall soon enter upon the continuing period of peace, a period when there will be no more war, when disputes between nations will be settled by the application of man's power of reason, by international law.

Linus Pauling

There must be, not a balance of power, but a community of power; not organized rivalries, but an organized common peace.

Woodrow Wilson

There is no salvation for civilization, or even the human race, other than the creation of a world government.

Albert Einstein

Is there a doubt whether a common government can embrace so large a sphere? Let experience solve it....It is well worth a fair and full experiment.

George Washington

* World federalists hold before us the vision of a unified mankind living in peace under a just world order....The heart of their program—a world under law—is realistic and attainable.   **U Thant**
former Secretary-General, United Nations

When Kansas and Colorado have a quarrel over the water in the Arkansas River they don't call out the National Guard in each state and go to war over it. They bring suit in the Supreme Court of the United States and abide by the decision. There isn't a reason in the world why we cannot do that internationally.

Harry S. Truman

It will be just as easy for nations to get along in a republic of the world as it is for you to get along in the republic of the United States.

Harry S. Truman

The question is not one of "surrendering" national sovereignty. The problem is not negative and does not involve giving up something we already have. The problem is positive—creating something we lack...but...imperatively need...—the extension of law and order into another field of human association which heretofore has remained unregulated and in anarchy.

Emery Reves
The Anatomy of Peace

Internationalism does not mean the end of individual nations. Orchestras don't mean the end of violins.

Golda Meir

The tough-minded...respect difference. Their goal is a world made safe for differences, where the United States may be American to the hilt without threatening the peace of the world, and France may be France, and Japan may be Japan on the same conditions.

Ruth Fulton Benedict

We have a vision that our land and our people will once again be strong in ways that make us proud.

Women's Peace Presence

* If a nation were willing to risk destruction for peace and truth, man as a human being rather than a brute would have reasserted himself. Humanity as a spiritual reality would live. Truth, decency, honor, courage would still live on earth in the midst of madness. In time, civilization could be rebuilt on firmer and more beautiful lines than ever. In a profound sense all the suffering and the travail of men might be redeemed.

A. J. Muste

I refuse to accept the cynical notion that nation after nation must spiral down a militaristic stairway into the hell of thermonuclear destruction.

Martin Luther King, Jr.

* We dip into the future, far as human eye can see,
See the vision of the world and all the wonder that shall be,
Hear the war-drum throb no longer, see the battle flags all furled
In the parliament of man, the federation of the world.

Alfred Lord Tennyson

E. Beyond War

In hundreds of ways, we are killing this planet. The bomb is just the easiest way. We have a dream, Katya and I, a dream that we might stop killing things and preparing to kill each other. A dream that we might start...preparing for life, the life of those who will come and live on this planet.

from the play *Peace Child*

The broad ultimate requirements of survival...are in essence...global disarmament, both nuclear and conventional, and the invention of political means by which the world can peacefully settle the issues that throughout history it has settled by war.

Jonathan Schell
The Fate of the Earth

...ideological differences and vested interests must be dealt with in nonmilitary terms.

New Frontiers Center Newsletter
Fall, Winter 1983

We cannot expect to dispose of armaments until we have a plan for the common safety.

Norman Cousins

The world, in freeing itself of one burden, the peril of extinction, must inevitably shoulder another: it must assume full responsibility for settling human differences peacefully.

Jonathan Schell
The Fate of the Earth

We need an Academy of Peace, not to do away with conflict, but to learn and teach how to creatively "manage" conflict.

Theodore M. Hesburgh

* What do I now see as the way out for the underdeveloped world? Not violence. Today established violence keeps millions of people in a subhuman situation. For the third world to turn to violence would be to declare that no alternative exists....I dream about the day when there will dawn for mankind a new civilization with justice and peace recognized as the essential values. For me that dream has validity because I believe in the power of truth and love. I believe in the work of God, who will not allow falsehood and hate to prevail among men for all time. So I shall continue my attempts to carry out concrete action looking toward justice and peace, confident that those values will prevail— perhaps tomorrow, perhaps the day after tomorrow.

Archbishop Dom Helder Camara

Our earth is but a small star in the great universe, yet of it we can make, if we choose, a planet unvexed by war, untroubled by hunger or fear, undivided by senseless distinctions of race, color or theory.

Stephen Vincent Benét

I have a dream...deeply rooted in the American dream...that my four little children will one day live in a nation where they will not be judged by the color of their skin but by the content of their character...that little black boys and black girls will be able to join hands with little white boys and white girls and walk together as sisters and brothers.

Martin Luther King, Jr.
August 1963

* I have the audacity to believe that people everywhere can have three meals a day for their bodies, education and culture for their minds, and dignity, equality and freedom for their spirits. I believe that what self-centered men have torn down men other-centered can build up. I still believe that one day mankind will bow before the altars of God and be crowned triumphant over war and bloodshed, and nonviolent redemptive goodwill proclaim the rule of the land.

Martin Luther King, Jr.
on receiving the Nobel Peace Prize

We envision a world where children face the future without the threat of nuclear war. We imagine nations cooperating to feed people with the money now spent on weapons. We seek reconciliation between ourselves and our Mother, the Earth. We want our national forests used to shelter *life* rather than ELF transmitters that signal submarines with nuclear missiles. We believe that a world at Peace is within our common reach.

Women's Peace Presence

* The great question is: Can global war now be outlawed from the world? If so, it would mark the greatest advance in civilization since the Sermon on the Mount. It would lift at one stroke the darkest shadow which has engulfed mankind from the beginning. It would not only remove fear and bring security—it would not only create new moral and spiritual values—it would produce an economic wave of prosperity that would raise the world's standard of living beyond anything ever dreamed of by man.

General Douglas MacArthur
1961

If I heard all the nuclear weapons were being dismantled, I'd feel so relieved and so happy. I'd do 200 cartwheels in a row.

Katy
Age 9
In the Nuclear Shadow: What Can the Children Tell Us?

It will be a great day when our schools get all the money they need and the air force has to hold a bake sale to buy a bomber.

Women's International League for Peace and Freedom

It'll be a great day when our day care centers have all the money they need and the navy has to hold a bake sale to buy battleships.

Anonymous

If we can change our priorities, achieve balance and understanding in our roles as human beings in a complete world, the coming era can well be that of a richer civilization, not its end.

Sigurd Olson

A federation of all humanity, together with a sufficient measure of social justice to ensure health, education, and a rough equality of opportunity, would mean such a release and increase of human energy as to open a new phase in human history.

H. G. Wells
The Outline of History

Why believe that we in 2010 have come to a "lasting peace"? Perhaps it is the conviction that there comes a time when the time has come, when what we human beings could not previously do we now can do, should do, must do. Paul Tillich called such historical moments a *kairos*, from the Greek meaning when the time is ripe. Such a *kairos* came during the nineteenth century with the abolition of slavery. Since then the world has not looked back. Ten years ago, in the year 2000, the joint resolution on world peace, signed by every member of the General Assembly of the United Nations, noted that "disagreement is inevitable but war is unacceptable." Today, no one is interested in looking back.

J. Edward Barrett
Peace 2010
Christian Science Monitor

I dream of giving birth to a child who will ask: "Mother, what was war?"

Eve Merriam

May there always be sunshine,
May there always be blue skies,
May there always be Mama,
May there always be me.

Russian boy
Age 5

When the voices of children are heard on the green
And laughing is heard on the hill,
My heart is at rest within my breast
And everything is still.

William Blake
Nurse's Song

Peace. The choice of a new generation.

Matt Bell
7th Grader

I can't wait for peace, can you?

Faunia Fox
Age 6

Ring out old shapes of foul disease,
Ring out the narrowing lust of gold;
Ring out the thousand wars of old,
Ring in the thousand years of peace.

Alfred Lord Tennyson

...Some day, men and women will rise, they will reach the mountain peak, they will meet big and strong and free, ready to receive, to partake, and to bask in the golden rays of love. What fancy, what imagination, what poetic genius can foresee even approximately the potentialities of such a force in the life of men and women.

Emma Goldman

* Someday, after we have mastered the winds, the waves, the tides and gravity, we shall harness for God the energies of love. Then for the second time in the history of the world, man will have discovered fire.

Pierre Teilhard de Chardin

ADDITIONS:

Author Index